THE LIFE AND TIMES OF EAMON DE VALERA

Text
CONSTANTINE FITZGIBBON

Illustrative Material
GEORGE MORRISON

GILL AND MACMILLAN

Published by
Gill and Macmillan Ltd
2 Belvedere Place
Dublin 1
and internationally through association with the
Macmillan Publishers Group

Printing history
5 4 3 2 1

Jacket design: Jarlath Hayes

7171 0657 8

Printed and Bound in the Republic of Ireland by
The Richview Press Limited, Dublin

CONTENTS

ACKNOWLEDGEMENTS

The illustrations in this book were compiled by George Morrison from his own collection. He acknowledges permission for the use of additional copyright material from:
The Irish Press, The Sunday Press, The Evening Press, Mr. J. Cashman, Mr. Tom Kennedy, Lensmen Limited, Associated Press, Radio Times BBC Hulton Picture Library, World Wide Photos, *The Irish Times, Independent Newspapers Limited,* the Bettmann Archive.

Every effort has been made to discover and acknowledge the copyright ownership of all illustrative material reproduced in this book. In the event of omission, the Publishers would be grateful for formal notification.

INTRODUCTION

THIS is not an attempt to write a brief biography of President Eamon de Valera. Indeed any attempt at brevity when discussing his long and complex public life since first he stepped on to the political stage in 1913 and, since 1916, was almost always in the centre of that Irish stage, must be automatically doomed to failure. For his life is inextricably bound up with the creation of modern Ireland, politically, economically, socially, linguistically and in the religious sphere. In some of these fields, he failed. In none was he perhaps totally successful. Yet the imprint of his convictions and ambitions is to be discerned in every aspect of Irish life. To imagine twentieth century Ireland without de Valera would be as fruitless as to try and envisage an Elizabethan England without the great queen or a French *grand siècle* with Louis XIV omitted. No more can his, or their, actions and re-actions be contemplated, as it were, in the abstract. His and his country's life are inextricably intertwined. His official biography* handles this complicated relationship in very considerable detail, even though at the time of its writing not all the facts were available, and some perhaps never will be. The reader who desires more detail is referred to that authoritative work, on which this writer has drawn for most of the facts that follow. The purpose of this introduction, then, is merely to set the stage for the illustrations, text and quotations.

What sort of a man is Eamon de Valera? He has had many, bitter enemies, in England, among Irish-Americans and not least in Ireland itself, yet one senses in their animosity towards him a measure of considerable respect, even if grudgingly given. Many disliked, and at times hated, de Valera: none despised him. It was Talleyrand, I believe, who said that the value of a man should be measured against the weight of his enemies, not his friends. In such a scales de Valera's personal value would be great indeed, and commensurate with an integrity of purpose that at times approximated to arrogance. Intimate friends he had few, if indeed any. His private life has been very private, concerned with his wife—there was never any breath of scandal in a country that relishes scandal—and, perhaps to a lesser extent, his children. Charming in manner, when he so chose, and witty on occasion, he was nevertheless the very antithesis of what Dr Johnson called 'the clubbable man'. He was not a teetotaller, but the idea of de Valera drinking and chatting with his friends, the idea of an 'unbuttoned' de Valera, is quite inconceivable. Among the highly gregarious and loquacious Irish, whether politicians or not, such reticence was remarkable, one might almost say awe-inspiring. It is said that we are loved for our weaknesses. De Valera does not appear to have had any such mundane human weaknesses. Yet he was capable of inspiring, and perhaps for this very reason, the most intense devotion among many of his compatriots. Had he shown any human failings it is probable that they would have rounded on him as they once rounded on the equally icy Parnell when the O'Shea divorce proved, to their simple minds, that the uncrowned king had betrayed their trust in his moral fibre.

There are certain aspects of Eamon de Valera's background and upbringing which would seem to be relevant to any understanding of his character, though the importance of any one of these can easily be overrated.

His father was a Spaniard, Juan Vivion de Valera, the particule implying at least a descent from the nobility, though he himself was a poor man. National generalizations are highly questionable, but it would seem at least a speculative possibility that his son inherited a certain austerity of character and manner, a rare quality among Irishmen, which was of Spanish origin.

Since his parents' marriage rapidly broke up, for financial and health reasons, and the boy was shipped back to the County Limerick, there to be brought up by his uncle and aunt, he had no real family life in his earliest, most formative years. Without mother or father, brothers or sisters, he was brought up as a sort of semi-orphan, though well cared for by his relations. This must have accentuated both self-reliance and perhaps introspection. From his very earliest years he had to make his own way in the world, to plough his own furrow. He was strong enough to cope with this loneliness, this lack of direct family support. He was,

Eamon de Valera, by the Earl of Longford and Thomas P. O'Neill, Dublin & London 1970, Boston 1971.

however, to remain very much a 'loner'. One direct result of this was that with political success, even the very limited success and prestige that immediately came his way as one of the two fighting commandants who had survived the Rising and the courts martial of 1916, the role that he chose among his peers—and, more important perhaps, that Michael Collins, Arthur Griffith and the others granted him—was that of the leader, not that of the colleague even on a *primus inter pares* basis. From then on, and for the rest of his life, he was entirely conscious of his unique position in Irish political life. Indeed he was fully and repeatedly prepared to safeguard and even to exploit this uniqueness in his country's interests both in the national and in the international fields. When his enemies said that he used his unique status, as President of Sinn Fein, as leader of the opposition in and after the Civil War, as Taoiseach (Prime Minister) and finally as President of the Republic to forward his own, personal ends, they both were and were not misjudging him. He identified himself, and above all the positions that he held, with Ireland, much as his contemporary, General de Gaulle, identified himself with France. The claim in itself is of course arrogant, but neither statesman was motivated by the cruder sort of self-interest.

And here another, formative strand from his childhood becomes relevant. His childhood, adolescence and early manhood were passed in poverty. The degree of poverty was not, by the standards of the time, excessive, let alone intolerable. Until approximately the turn of the century when the Irish economy began slowly to improve, poverty was the normal lot of the Irish countryman, particularly in the west. It was this poverty which had driven his mother, like so many others, to seek a living as a domestic servant in the United States. Being so general, there was no shame attached to such poverty, nor was de Valera's family among the very poorest. Indeed Irish poverty was blamed, and in large measure correctly, on the maladministration of the British authorities and of their 'rooted garrison', the landlord class and their agents. It would be an exaggeration to say poverty in late nineteenth century Ireland was a badge of patriotism—many of the Irish leaders in the coming Anglo-Irish struggle were of middle class and not infrequently of Protestant origin—but no more was it a disgrace in a country that had been spoliated by its English conquerors for three and more centuries. Since Ireland had never known feudalism save marginally, and that as an alien and short-lived importation, no true class hierarchy had struck roots outside, perhaps, of the Pale, nor had American plutocratic values then impinged on the agricultural west. This was one reason why the Anglo-Irish struggle, far more so than the Irish Civil War that followed, was not at all a class war. Men of the most humble background, though perhaps of ancient lineage, such as Collins or de Valera could and did mix as equals, and indeed lead, men who came from what the English and to a lesser extent the Americans would then and perhaps now regard as a 'higher' social class. De Valera had, in fact, no reason to feel ashamed of his financial and social background, nor did he at any time give the slightest indication of any such despicably tragic self-pity.

A boy brought up in circumstances of poverty can either surrender to circumstance—that is to say, with whatever tacit mental and emotional reservations he may care to make, accept his status as a member of the proletariat or peasantry —or he can use his abilities and energies to escape from that status. This will usually, but by no means invariably, take the form of making money. This has certainly been true of many Irishmen, born without privilege, since the days when de Valera was a boy. However in every generation, everywhere, there are poor young men for whom wealth as such is not the prime attraction. And there are periods of history, in every country, in which knowledge, and through knowledge ultimate power, provide a far more attractive magnet. This is perhaps particularly true of a revolutionary, or pre-revolutionary, situation. De Valera had little in common with Robespierre, yet he too was a 'sea-green incorruptible'. During his long political career it would not have been difficult for him to amass, quite legally, a fortune, as some of his successors have done. Yet he retired, full of honours, a comparatively poor man. And the answer to this class problem is easy: wealth simply did not interest him.

A boy from his background could only hope to let his character and his potential abilities develop through education, and this in turn meant the winning of scholarships in an age when medium and higher education was far from being a universal prerogative. These he won, though not always and not easily. His *forte* was mathematics, and this fact he seems to have realised at a comparatively early age. Though quite well read in the humanities, and a Gaelic scholar of very considerable distinction, the young Eamon de Valera turned the searchlight of his mind, as it were, on to the abstract concepts of higher mathematics. This totally unemotional, pure study must have appealed to him precisely for the reasons of his childhood and upbringing that I have attempted briefly to outline in previous pages. Here there was, and could be, no human emotion involved, as there must have been had he devoted his mind to the liberal arts. Here, like every other mathematician, he was alone with the symbols of what he regarded as reality. Though this writer is incapable of judgment, I have heard that he had the makings of a mathematician of the very first eminence, another Bertrand Russell for example, perhaps even an Einstein. Though both those great men became ultimately, for better or for worse, involved in politics of the greatest importance, it is safe to assume that neither of them envisaged their training in abstractions as a preliminary to political activity. Such was certainly the case with de Valera. Mathematics was, and remained, his passionate intellectual activity and its own especial disciplines affected his thoughts on other matters, but it is safe to say that in his youth he never regarded it as a lever to political power. Nor was it. Since 1916 he had, particularly in times of distress, found refuge in the reading of mathematics: he did not, to the best of this writer's knowledge, ever write down his mathematical beliefs.

Another aspect of de Valera's character which is of the greatest possible importance but concerning which, throughout his long life, he has been even by his own standards exceptionally discreet is his religion. That he is a devout believer, and constantly aware of his Christian duties, goes without saying. He treated the Princes of the Church, and more humble clerics and monastics of both sexes, with the greatest respect: the visitors' book of the Presidential Lodge is enough to show how much time he was prepared to give to churchmen, both Irish and foreign, and there is every evidence that he usually enjoyed and relished their company, conversation and advice. He, perhaps more than any other prominent Irishman of his generation, saw to it that the Roman Catholic Church and its hierarchy assumed for a time a position of great importance and influence in Irish public life which in twentieth century Europe has scarcely been surpassed, even in General Franco's Spain or President Salazar's Portugal. It was, until 1972 the State Church though the constitution merely gave it a special position, but was inbred with an independence that even the Bourbon kings never granted to the Gallican Church in France.

Yet despite his devotion to his Church—his official biographers state that during his Presidency he was in the habit of attending his private chapel as often as five times a day—and despite the great power that he exercised in a predominantly Roman Catholic country, with only quite brief intervals, over half a century, he never allowed his religious convictions to influence, either in his public or his private life, his attitude towards Christians of other faiths. Neither Sinn Féin, nor the Free State nor the Republic over which he presided was ever overtly used for sectarian purposes, as for example was the Orange Order in Northern Ireland. A contributory factor to this almost ecumenical nature of the Irish state may have been the fact that during the Civil War, of 1922–1923, the Republicans, of whom de Valera was a most prominent member, were refused the sacraments, an order by the hierarchy which was only in part obeyed by the priesthood. De Valera never commented on this, an obvious major tragedy in his own spiritual life. It would however not be injudicious to assume that this experience must have reinforced him in what he probably already knew: that religious doctrine and political theory do not make comfortable or easy alliances. Secondly, since from an early age he regarded himself as the representative of the Irish people, of all the Irish people, he could not cast out those of his compatriots who did not worship God in his own Church, all the more so since the names of his closest colleagues included such Protestants as Hyde, Casement, Barton and Childers. He handled this most delicate matter with the greatest possible skill, and to the lasting benefit of his country. In a word, he prized democracy above theocracy.

All Irishmen? At the time of writing the Border is still with us, and there is a plethora of misery to the North, with another civil war, even another Anglo-Irish war, spluttering along its dynamite trail. When the last Civil War took place, the great mathematician thought to formulise it in his refusal to accept allegiance to 'the Crown'. Later, he changed his mind, a very rare occurrence, and found a formula for this purpose too. He was, both in 1922 and when he accepted at last the Oath to the Crown nearly a decade later, disingenuous. The Civil War was about partition, in so far as it was about any major issue other than political power in the new Free State, and de Valera both failed to say this and lost the war: Partition is with us still, solidified by the passage of time. He never became the acknowledged leader of all Ireland.

His other, though perhaps less important, failure was the Irish language. This writer is well aware of the immense importance of linguistics to national identity. An Irish-speaking, or even a bilingual, Ireland would be from every point of view a far stronger entity than an Anglo-American-speaking Ireland. Immense effort, including I am told 38 per cent of the school children's time, has been devoted to this endeavour. It has failed, and the children forget their Irish (save in order to get civil service jobs) as fast as ever they can. This is not de Valera's fault, nor that of those other brave men who took pride in their nationality. The point of no return had been reached before their time, perhaps at the period of the Famine and the massive emigration that followed, perhaps even earlier. Other European languages have vanished in modern times, Burgundian and Provençal to name but two, but perhaps none so beautiful and elegant as that of the Irish. Its revival was a valiant attempt that failed. The world is the poorer.

The pictures, and the text, that follow are an attempt to show the man who tried, with considerable success and considerable failure, to create or revive a country that had been conquered, smothered and almost destroyed. It exists, and he was its midwife at its rebirth, though it is not a realisation of his and his friends' young dreams. Goethe once remarked that we always get what we passionately desire: but too late. Perhaps we shall one day see the Ireland that de Valera desired so passionately; perhaps it may not even be too late; more probably never.

C.F.

PART ONE

Sod cabin of the 1860s

THIS undated photograph of a turf cottage was probably taken some time before Eamon de Valera's birth, in the west or southwest of Ireland. It exemplifies the extreme poverty of rural Ireland, especially Munster and Connaught, which had led to the Great Famine of the late 1840s and early 1850s and was only ameliorated by the Land Act of 1881 and subsequent acts that slowly improved the wretched countryman's lot. Note the unshod man lying on the cabin's roof.

It was from such abject poverty, from an Ireland which had almost no industry to offer alternative employment, that vast numbers of often embittered emigrants fled abroad, to England, to Australia, but above all to the United States and Canada, throughout the second half of the nineteenth century and well into the twentieth. Eamon de Valera's mother, Catherine Coll, was of their number. Her childhood home, near Bruree, Co. Limerick, was not as brutally impoverished as the one shown in this photograph, but she saw such scenes, and after her father's death, when she was seventeen, emigration seemed at last the only choice.

Thomas Francis Meagher and William Smith O'Brien in gaol the day before their sentence of death was commuted to transportation, 1848. On the right is the gaoler

ENGLISH rule in Ireland was very close to naked expropriation and was described by the Frenchman, Stendhal, as the worst in Europe—not excluding Sicily. The alternative to emigration was the overthrow of British rule either by constitutional means, as had been attempted by Daniel O'Connell in the second quarter of the nineteenth century with no success, or by revolutionary methods. These alternatives formed the constant swing of the Irish political pendulum from the time of the Act of Union (1800) until the Treaty that established the Irish Free State in 1922. It continues to swing in that part of Ireland still ruled from London at the time of writing. It vitally affected the whole of Eamon de Valera's public life.

The first rising of any historical importance, since that of Robert Emmet in 1803, was organised by the group of patriots called Young Ireland, in 1848, the Year of Revolution in all Europe. A starving populace, in the grip of the Great Famine, failed to respond. The leaders fled abroad or were captured. Two of them, William Smith O'Brien and Thomas Francis Meagher, were condemned to death, though this was later commuted and they were transported to Australia. The photograph on the facing page was taken in prison the night before the death sentence was commuted, the man on their left being a prison official.

The story of Young Ireland must have been well-known to Catherine Coll. Certainly her son numbered these patriotic rebels among his heroes.

Jeremiah O'Donovan Rossa, c.1885

Kilmainham Gaol

PHYSICALLY and politically Young Ireland was entirely destroyed: emotionally and morally it quite rapidly revived, for the phoenix of Irish patriotism has always stretched its wings upon the ashes of disaster. Its new incarnation was in the Fenians, later almost invariably referred to as the Irish Republican Brotherhood or I.R.B., and frequently called, quite simply, the Organisation. It was a secret society, non-sectarian and virtually classless, dedicated to the overthrow, by means including violence, of British rule in Ireland and thence to the establishment of an all-Irish Republic. Beyond that it had no programme of social reform, though the return of Irish land to Irish owners was implicit.

One of the best known of the earlier Fenians was O'Donovan Rossa (1831–1915) whose adopted last name was derived from Rosscarbery in Co. Cork, where he was born in what is now the post office of that pleasant little town. Arrested for Fenian activities in the failed uprising of 1867, he was elected to the United Kingdom parliament while serving a long sentence in an English jail in 1869 after incarceration, like so many other Fenian leaders, in Kilmainham Gaol, thus establishing a precedent that de Valera was to follow half a century later. He lived to a great age and his funeral, in 1915, was the occasion of a spectacular display of Irish patriotism. The oration was delivered by Pádraig Pearse and was, perhaps, his greatest piece of oratory. Among those who heard it was Eamon de Valera, already a member, though an inactive one, of the I.R.B.

Smashed as a result of the events of 1867, the I.R.B. was revived almost immediately in America, in 1873. For many years its leader was John Devoy (1842–1928). The Irish in America had prospered and were soon rich enough to be the financial supporters of Irish republicanism in the old country.

During his sojourn in America, from June 1919 to December 1920, de Valera was to quarrel with Devoy whose views on policy were too conservative and too cautious for the younger man's taste.

A British Army barracks, Ireland, c.1860–1868 (above)

An eviction; note military and Royal Irish Constabulary (left)

Land League huts built to house the evicted (below)

THE economic background in rural Ireland, both before Eamon de Valera's birth and during his childhood, is of the greatest importance. Since there was virtually no industry and very little commerce apart from the eastern areas, from Belfast to Cork, the economy of Ireland meant agriculture. After the Repeal of the Corn Laws by the United Kingdom parliament (1846) and, even more, the massive exportation of American corn crops that followed the vast tillage of the United States' Middle West, only briefly halted by the Civil War there (1861–65), agriculture in Ireland became, in a *laissez-faire* economy, increasingly pastoral. Therefore far fewer farm labourers were needed to tend cows than had been needed to grow corn: therefore the landlords were anxious to be rid of a portion of their peasant tenantry: therefore, when the tenants refused to leave their homes for which they could no longer pay the rent—evictions. These were often carried out with great brutality, the actual home of those evicted being demolished by the Royal Irish Constabulary and the military, as is shown in the photograph opposite.

The Irish reacted, and the Land War resulted. The weapons of the Irish were 'boycott' and 'no rent'. The Land League came into existence, to fight the landlords and their agents. It was popular, but again had little social ideology, other than that the land of Ireland belonged by every moral right to the people of Ireland. The Land League even built huts in which to house the evicted tenants. Its greatest leader was Michael Davitt and it, and its enemies, infused yet more bitterness into the Irish scene into which Eamon de Valera was to grow up. From every point of view, neutrality was becoming impossible.

Michael Davitt, c.1882

Charles Stewart Parnell, c.1880

AGRARIAN unrest had been endemic in the Irish countryside for centuries. With the partial collapse of the landlord system and the evictions it became more acute and was, as it were, organised and indeed institutionalised by Davitt's Land League created in 1879 to fight the landlords with the ultimate intention of land nationalisation.

Davitt was a Fenian. His family had been evicted from their Mayo home when he was four years old. From 1870 to 1877 he was in an English prison for Fenian activities. He gave the Irish resistance to British rule a modern, social, even moderately socialistic, content which had been lacking since the time of Wolfe Tone, the United Irishmen and the French revolutionary influence of the 1790s.

Parnell, a Protestant aristocrat, was not in that sense a revolutionary at all. The 'uncrowned King of Ireland' from 1879 until the O'Shea divorce scandal toppled him in 1890, he was essentially a parliamentarian prepared to use the British constitution to encompass its own overthrow in Ireland. He was not a 'physical force' man, but was prepared to work with any group of Irish patriots not committed to terrorism. He was thus in alliance with Davitt and with the Irish-Americans. During his 'kingship' he moulded Irish resistance into a coherent and very credible force which crumbled with his fall, but left its powerful legend.

Eamon de Valera was a boy of almost nine when Parnell died. His mother, Catherine Coll, known as Kate, was born in 1856. At the age of twenty-three, in that same year of 1879, she emigrated to New York where she had an aunt living in Brooklyn.

There she obtained employment as a domestic servant and it was while working for the Giraud family, in the children's nursery, that she met her future husband, Vivion de Valera, who it seems was employed by the family to give music lessons to the children. The Girauds, of French origin, were members of New York high society of that period, civilised and therefore interested in the arts.

De Valera's mother, Catherine, née Coll, c.1885

West 42nd Street from Park Avenue, New York City, at the turn of the century

VIVION de Valera was a Spaniard whose father was engaged in the Cuba-Spain sugar trade. He had been a sculptor until eye damage made this an impossibility, then an accountant, and finally a music teacher. They married in September of 1881 and a little over a year later their only child was born.

Vivion de Valera suffered from poor health, and it may be from him that his son inherited the defective eye-sight that led to cataracts and culminated in near total blindness. The father may also have suffered from what was then called consumption. The climate of New York was too unhealthy, and he was forced, in 1884, to go to Denver, Colorado, leaving his wife and baby son in New York. A year later he was dead.

The child had been christened Edward, but once he entered Irish public life he preferred the Irish version of that name. Both his parents were devout Roman Catholics, their marriage and the baptism of their child being celebrated in the Church of their faith.

Queenstown (now Cobh) Co. Cork, c.1882

*The Coll house near Bruree,
Co. Limerick, as it was*

THE widowed Mrs de Valera had no choice but to go back to work. The baby boy was cared for by another Bruree immigrant to New York, a Mrs Doyle. His earliest memory of his mother was of a lady in black who came to visit him. This arrangement was not satisfactory and it was decided that his uncle Ned Coll should take him back to Ireland, to live with his grandmother, his Uncle Pat and his Aunt Hannie.

He landed at Queenstown near Cork, so named because Queen Victoria, like little Eddie de Valera, had there first set foot on Irish soil. (It has reverted to its ancient name of Cobh.) The fact that de Valera had been born in the United States, and therefore could claim American citizenship though he never did, contributed marginally to the fact that he was not executed after the 1916 Easter Rising.

The day after his arrival the Coll family moved into their new home near Bruree. This was one of the first agricultural cottages built by the Liberal government as part of a re-housing programme. His Uncle Pat was a very small farmer. Among the little boy's earliest political memories were the clearing of Parnell's name at the time of the Pigott forgeries (1888) and the boycotting at about the same time of an unpopular local landlord.

William Ewart Gladstone, c. First Home Rule Bill, 1886

Lord Randolph Churchill, 1885

THROUGHOUT the second half of the 1880s parliamentary politics were in the forefront of Irish public life. Parnell was at the height of his power and Gladstone had declared his Liberal Party in favour of Home Rule, partly for high moral principles, and in part because he needed the support of the Irish members at Westminster. His first Home Rule Bill, however, was defeated in 1886 and his government fell.

It was during this campaign that a new and bitter factor was injected into the Irish problem, when Lord Randolph Churchill decided 'to play the Orange card'. This meant that sectarian bitterness in Ulster was given a sort of political respectability in that it was henceforth to be used for English party-political ends. This—'Ulster will fight and Ulster will be right'—has bedevilled all attempts to find a happy all-Irish solution from that day to this. Ulster, however, is far from Bruree, and certainly the little boy cannot have guessed that in years to come his country and he personally would have to pay a very heavy price for Lord Randolph's cynical opportunism.

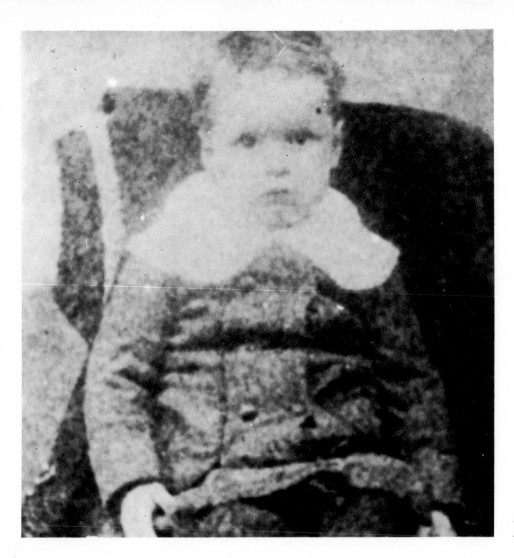

Earliest authenticated photograph of Eamon de Valera aged 2½ years

DE VALERA'S mother visited him in Bruree, at about the time when he was about four and a half years old. Quite soon she returned to America, where she married Charles Wheelwright, Uncle Charlie to the de Valera boy. Eamon de Valera's half-brother was to become a priest, a Redemptorist who as an American intervened on his behalf with the President of the United States when de Valera was condemned to death by a British court-martial in 1916.

His Aunt Hannie, too, had emigrated to America while he was still a baby, though she returned a few years later to care for her mother in Mrs Coll's old age and sickness. Thus the boy was really brought up by his grandmother and his Uncle Pat. Uncle Pat had political views which led him into the Land and Labour League.

Though poor, he was a respected figure, and was one of the Poor Law Guardians for the Kilmallock area. (The market town of Kilmallock is some four miles from the village of Bruree.) De Valera's childhood was therefore typical of that of Irish rural children of the poor (but not the poorest) class, quite well educated and politically conscious. Years later he was to say that when he wished to know what the people of Ireland were thinking he only had to look into his own heart. So far as the rural population went this was less a boast than a statement of fact. Despite his Spanish father and his American birth, he passed his childhood in circumstances that might be described as archetypal for Irish country boys of his generation and indeed of generations that preceded and succeeded his own.

Charleville (now Rathluirc) Co. Limerick, c.1898

De Valera, shortest standing, and Brother Prenderville, head teacher, Rathluirc (Charleville) school

IN 1888 his formal schooling began. He first went, for eight years, to the village school at Bruree, walking there and back, a distance of one mile each way, by Irish standards not a long walk even for a small boy of six or seven.

The year 1896 was a critical one for the boy. On the one hand his Uncle Pat was about to be married and the boy wished to get away from Bruree, all the more since his closest friend had moved on to the Christian Brothers' school in Charleville. He therefore asked his mother to have him brought to America, but nothing came of this. On the other hand, at the age of 14, either his education must finish—in which case he could only become a farm labourer, since his first steps towards emigration had come to nothing —or receive further education at his family's expense or by means of scholarships. This, in fact, was the decision reached. He followed his friend, Paddy Shea, to the Christian Brothers' school at Charleville in November, 1896, where he studied for two years. His Uncle Pat could not afford a bicycle for the boy. He therefore walked seven miles each way to the school, laden down with his schoolbooks. He worked hard, did well in his examinations, and thus won for himself the possibilities of higher education.

From his early youth, heredity apart, Eamon de Valera has been in the very best sense of the phrase 'a self-made man'. Perhaps as a result he was always to be remarkably adverse to intellectual or moral pressure from others, often of more flamboyant personality, whether these were to be friends or enemies in his political life, Irishmen or foreigners. The pride of those who have ploughed a straight furrow is obvious, sometimes overbearing: but in great men, and perhaps especially among devoutly religious men, it is sometimes accompanied by a personal humility that often appears to others as perhaps incompatible with moral and intellectual certainty.

Tim Healy M.P., 1855–1931, later Governor-
General of the Irish Free State (above)

Dr Eoin MacNeill, c.1893 (top left)

John Dillon, M.P. c.1890 (left)

WITH the fall of Parnell, which some would describe as his betrayal by part of the priesthood and of the people, with the I.R.B. dormant if not actually a moribund society of aging men, and with much of the vigour being taken out of the Land League by sensible, agricultural reforms that were eventually to hand over the land of Ireland to the men who worked it, Ireland in the 1890s was politically tranquil.

Politics, during de Valera's late adolescence and early manhood did not, of course, cease but became muted as Irish patriotism shifted, temporarily, to the 'cultural' and even the sporting field. On the one hand there was the great literary and theatrical revival known, not quite correctly, as 'the Celtic Renaissance'. The writers were usually men of Protestant, Anglo-Irish descent: Yeats, AE. (Russell), Synge, Stephens, Lady Gregory and many more in that nest of singing birds that was in some measure to be exemplified by the Abbey Theatre in Dublin. On the other hand they derived much of their material and indeed their viewpoint from the older, ancient Irish, culture that still lingered on among countrymen in the west and south. They were helped to do this—for few of them were themselves Irish speakers in origin —by the vigorous attempts of such Irish scholars as Dr Douglas Hyde (1860–1949), a Protestant who was to become the first President of the Irish Republic, and Dr Eoin MacNeill (1867–1945). Both were to achieve great prominence in the struggle to come. In 1893 they had founded the Gaelic League, to preserve and revitalise the Irish language: it was, however, not until 1908 that de Valera joined the Central Branch, Ard-Chraobh, of the League.

Nine years earlier in 1884, the Gaelic Athletic Association had come into existence. This, too, was a nationalist organisation, dedicated to the playing of traditional Irish games, such as hurling, rather than games imported from England, such as cricket or rugby. The G.A.A.'s appeal was to a different age group and, usually, to men of a different intellectual status from the Gaelic League, though many young nationalists were members of both, and both were eventually to be more or less controlled or at least heavily infiltrated by the revived I.R.B. of the early twentieth century.

The parliamentary situation was confused, and the Irish M.P.s split, once Parnell had gone. The anti-Parnellite faction was headed by John Dillon (1851–1927), and Tim Healy (1855–1931): the latter was to become the first Irish Governor-General of the Irish Free State. The leader of the Parnellites, since 1900 of virtually all the Irish Party at Westminster, was John Redmond (1856–1918). By the 1890s these parliamentarians had ceased to be 'physical force' men, though Dillon at least had a fiery past in the Land League days. Both wings voted with the Liberals for the Home Rule Bill proposed by Gladstone during his last administration in 1893. Passed by the House of Commons, it was massively defeated in the House of Lords. For nearly twenty years thereafter it was a dead letter, and the Irish M.P.s in the United Kingdom parliament had little to occupy them save constitutional, normal party-political procedure. Gradually they lost the leadership, and even the respect, of the younger generation of Irish republican nationalists, influenced by the Gaelic League and the G.A.A., and a member of this generation was Eamon de Valera. John Redmond was a decent gentleman and a most honest patriot, as were almost all his followers: he was, however, quite lacking in those charismatic qualities so marked in Parnell and in some of Redmond's successors.

De Valera (holding book) at Blackrock College

The old castle building, Blackrock College, as it was at the time of de Valera's presence there in the 1890s

AT the age of fifteen, in 1898, de Valera passed his junior grade examination with honours in all subjects (which did not include history). This entitled him to a small scholarship, £20 per annum, which, provided he worked and passed further examinations, as he did, enabled him to attend Blackrock College near Dublin, a school run by the Holy Ghost Fathers where he studied for a further five years. The purpose of these studies was to become either a priest or a school-master.

It was at Blackrock that he discovered a marked aptitude for mathematics, a subject for which he developed a veritable passion that was to last throughout his life. He therefore decided, on the advice of his clerical school masters, to become a teacher rather than a priest.

It was extremely difficult at that time for a Roman Catholic without private means to attend an Irish, or any other, university. Nor did he do so. However his grades and honours at Blackrock were high enough for him to be appointed in 1903 teacher of mathematics to the senior boys at Rockwell College, near Cashel, Co. Tipperary, which was also run by the Holy Ghost Fathers. He remained there only for a mere two years, for he found the provincial atmosphere stagnant.

He enjoyed athletics, and indeed obtained a local reputation both as a runner and a player of Rugby football (so he was not then a member of the G.A.A.) His political views, if they existed at all, were very moderate both at Blackrock and at Rockwell. In the first school's debating society he spoke, both against the French Revolution, which views he doubtless gleaned from his teacher-priests, and—a little more surprising—in favour of monarchy. He was, in fact, devoting his very considerable mental faculties to obtaining a university degree by methods which would nowadays be called a correspondence course.

British troops in Limerick, c.1896

THE comparative, and indeed un-usual, placidity of Irish political life was, at the time, briefly and irrelevantly interrupted by the Boer War (1899–1902). Here was a small foreign nation fighting, and at first winning victories against, the greatest imperial power that the world had seen since Rome's Empire. British troops were moved from Ireland to fight the embattled farmers in South Africa.

A few hundred Irishmen drew certain obvious conclusions from this apparent evidence of Britain's military inefficiency. A few score made their way to South Africa and fought with the Boers against the common enemy and traditional oppressor. One of these was John MacBride.

In Ireland itself Fenian embers were soon to be fanned, in part by a new generation arising in a new century, in part by the lessons of this Boer War, and also in part by the failure of the Irish Party to achieve Irish freedom through parliamentary methods. The I.R.B. came to life again, if only slowly and instructed by earlier, now aged, Fenians in the first decade of the twentieth century.

Countess Markievicz, née Constance Gore-Booth, c.1897 (top left)

Major John MacBride, 1915 (centre)

Pre-1914 portrait of Maud Gonne (MacBride) (bottom left)

W. B. Yeats, c.1906 (above)

Sir Roger Casement, c.1910 (below)

THE actors who were to play their parts in the drama to come now were appearing upon the stage, though often in curious disguise. Maud Gonne (1865–1953), was to marry John MacBride, and to become as dedicated a fighter for Irish freedom as was he. W. B. Yeats (1865–1939) was to fall in love with this proud and beautiful woman.

The Countess Markievicz (1868–1927), née Gore-Booth, was an ornament of Irish high society both before and after her marriage to her somewhat feckless, charming Polish Count. Later she was to become an extreme socialist and to fight the English as a soldier in uniform. Roger Casement (1864–1916) was in 1910 a retired British civil servant. An Ulsterman, a Protestant and probably a homosexual, he was to be knighted for his great humanitarian work in the Belgian Congo and in South America. He accepted the knighthood but not the accolade, and he too became an extreme activist among the Irish patriots.

Arthur Griffith, as a young man

Arthur Griffith's paper, 1907

Sinn Féin

DUBLIN, MARCH 9th, 1907.

showing that we are relatively the most heavily-taxed people in the world, taxed for being kept in subjection and being kept between the jail and the workhouse —taxed to keep a crowd of importations to manage our own affairs. In 1871 the number of persons incapacitated from employment for want of food, and who were obliged to resort to the necessity of seeking Poor Law Relief, was 69,791. According to the official statement of the year 1904, that number had reached 102,000, thus showing an increase of 32,209. Now, let it be perfectly understood, that we cannot and do not charge the Irish Parliamentary Party with being directly responsible for this state of affairs in Ireland ; but I contend that by attending the House of Commons and consequently recognising the right of a foreign assembly to make laws to bind the people of Ireland, and of conducting our national affairs, that they are indirectly responsible, and that they are wasting a sum of £25,000 per annum which might be properly devoted to national development, or certainly to some other purpose than helping to keep us serfs. Now, dropping the question of nationality for the moment altogether, can they justify their own policy as being the correct policy to pursue? Speaking fundamentally of their policy, their express purpose is to procure a measure of Home Rule, and this measure of Home Rule is to be the foundation-stone on which the Irish nation is to be built—built intellectually, nationally, and physically. Well, from a national point of view, nothing can be done for the country until they procure Home Rule,

The branch will hold its first public meeting at the rooms, Dolphin's Barn-street, on Monday, March 11th, on which date an address will be delivered by P. S. Ua Muincacháin, entitled " The Sinn Fein Idea in the Nineteenth Century," with special reference to the present movement. The address will be followed by a discussion in which visitors (who are cordially invited) will be entitled to take part. The sessional programme of the branch will be announced as soon as finally arranged. Names of intending members will be taken by the secretary on Monday night.

Cork.

A public meeting in furtherance of the policy of Sinn Fein was held on Friday evening in the Council Chamber, City Hall. It was organised by the local National Council.

Mr. E. Sheehan, M.A., presided, and there was a large attendance.

The Chairman congratulated the meeting on its attendance, and the local branch of the Sinn Féin movement on the numbers who had come in already and become members of their branch. The man who professed ardent patriotism and still refused to join the national organisations and work as a unit by the side of others to help on their cause, such a man was no Nationalist at all. He therefore urged all who believed in their principles to become active members and help to advance their movement. That movement, instead of being a new-fangled one, based on mystical and far-fetched ideas, was on the contrary based on the solid prin-

doing so, a debate was arranged, but when the hour arrived for putting their talk to the test of reason, the men were not to be found, with the exception of one unassuming man no other could be found to stand up for the " floor of the House " weapon. The men who have most to say against the Sinn Fein idea are shrewd enough to avoid the risk of losing their cheap reputation for debate in defending a discredited policy. Last week an election came off in the Tower Ward which proved beyond doubt, if even there was a shadow of doubt about the kind of chameleon-like thing that calls itself the United Irish League. The National Council, in accordance with its usual custom, submitted a list of questions to the rival candidates, Messrs. O'Hanlon and Murray. The former agreed with the National Council on every point raised, and pledged himself to give effect to his promise when occasion would demand, while the latter though agreeing to five of the queries was not opposed to emigration and the presentation of loyal addresses to representatives of British rule in Ireland. The Sinn Fein party decided, therefore, to support Mr. O'Hanlon, who is a good Nationalist ; he is also a member of the U.I.L. But the members of that organisation worked against their fellow-member and claimed the Unionist vote, which happened to be strong in this Ward, on the strength of Mr. Murray favouring loyal addresses ! The cabal which rules municipal affairs in Waterford at present are Mr. J. Redmond's chief supporters—they are the same unprincipled gang who

the following measures to the Irish people ; That they issue at least 50 per cent. of the capital in £10 stock in Ireland and allocate it solely to Irish purchasers ; that they confer power on the General Council of County Councils to nominate a National Director invested with powers on behalf of this country ; that a duly executed agreement be arrived at between the promoters and the General Council on the matter of importation of Canadian cattle ; that wayleave should be paid to the County Councils ; equal recognition of the Irish language with the English ; use of Irish materials as far as possible ; and that the headquarters of the Board be situated in Ireland. We maintain this should be Ireland's minimum price for the use of her harbours and highways. Copies to be sent to the County and District Councils of Mayo." It was decided that the yearly subscriptions be received at next meeting, when a subscription list will be opened in support of the Executive Council of the Organisation. Mr. John Hoban was elected vice-president of the branch. The meeting was unanimous that the branch would take part in the St. Patrick's Day Demonstration organised by the Gaelic League. A number of membership cards having been distributed, the meeting adjourned.

Kilmore.

A meeting of the branch was held in Courthouse, Ballinagh, Mr. P. M'Mahon, president in the chair. He congratulated the members on the progress made, and said the National Council was

THE GAELIC LEAGUE.

Dublin Feis, 1907.

The following dates have been provisionally fixed for the various competitions : Saturday, 13th April, Public Competitions in Rotunda—Choral, Dancing, and Junior Singing and Recitation ; Intermediate and National Schools Interclass competitions. Tuesday, 16th April —Branch Inter-class, 1st and 2nd years. Wednesday, 17th April—Senior Singing and Recitation Competitions. Friday, 19th April—Branch Inter-class, 3rd, 4th, and 5th years. Saturday, 20th April—Individual Language and History Competitions ; Extra Schools and Classes Competitions. Wednesday, 24th April—Cuirm Ceoil na Feise.

"Movement" and "Language" in Belfast.

The general returns of the last Language Fund Collection show that with the natural exception of Dublin, Belfast contributed far more than any other centre. Workers in the capital of "foreignism" in Ireland expect, however, that this year's fund will greatly exceed last year's. The Coiste Ceanntair has by its enterprise in the taking of commodious premises, the holding of important public meetings, the establishment of its very successful Training College for Irish teachers, and so on shown that it is deserving of support in its work for the nation ; language fund Belfast people appreciate such support and will contribute accordingly.

It would appear, also, as if the dis-

ARTHUR Griffith (1872–1922) was a highly talented journalist and writer. In 1899, after his return from South Africa, he founded his newspaper *The United Irishman*. Later renamed *Sinn Féin* (usually translated as 'ourselves' or 'we alone') it led to the creation of the political movement of that name early in the new century.

Griffith belongs somewhere near the middle of the Irish politico-revolutionary spectrum. He was not a 'physical force' extremist, at least before 1916, but in view of the failure of Gladstone and the Liberals to implement their promise of Home Rule, he believed, as the name of his paper and his party implied, that the Irish must work out their own salvation rather than rely on the benevolence of the United Kingdom parliament and the work of the Irish M.P.s therein.

Essentially a constitutionalist, he advocated a system based on the model of the Austro-Hungarian dual monarchy. Nevertheless, and almost despite himself, his party was to become the embodiment of the Irish Revolution of 1916. By then he had, with great grace and generosity, handed over the presidency of Sinn Féin to Eamon de Valera.

James Connolly

James Connolly's weekly, 1898

THE WORKERS' Republic

Ir dóig linn gur mór iad na "daoine-móra" map atamaoid féin ap ár nglúnaib, éingmir

VOL. I. No 4.   DUBLIN, SEPTEMBER 3, 1898   WEEKLY, ONE PENNY.

Home Thrusts.

The compositor fiend had his innings last week. Whether it was revolutionary enthusiasm or loyalist spleen which disturbed his brain we know not, but we do know that pages 3 and 7 and part of page 6 of our last issue presented to the readers a new species of grammar and orthography decidedly unknown to the writers of this paper.

      * *

The spelling was as vile as the principles of a hireling scribe on an Unionist or Home Rule newspaper, and the grammar was as doubtful as the patriotism of a politician.

      * *

We are assured by the printer that precautions have been taken to prevent the recurrence of such mistakes. We hope so.

list of toasts, *An Irish Republic*; would the loyalists present have sat in silence or allowed their names to go to the newspapers as participating in the function?

      * *

And if they had would *their* newspapers have remained silent over the matter as our Home Rule rags have done?

      * *

Is it too much to expect that our Nationalist politicians (so-called) shall at least be as consistent in their public actions as the Unionists whom they pretend to oppose?

      * *

Does not the howl set up by all those middle-class journalists when any of their number is exposed and their little treacheries held up to the light of day, betray an uneasy conscience?

      * *

But *United Ireland* wants the Workers'

Home Rule Editors drinking loyal toasts to-day and writing "patriotic articles" to-morrow, Home Rule Corporations electing Tory Lord Mayors, the conquest of Ireland at last accepted and ratified by her sons.

      * *

Said Darby the Blast in Lever's novel, "Tom Burke of Ours," "Bad luck to the gintry, 'tis the gintry ever and always betrayed us."

      + +

Since our Home Rule politicians were graciously permitted to associate with Lords and Earls on the Financial Relations agitation, all the virility and aggressiveness has gone out of our public life, and our politicians are now afraid to utter a single sentence which might not suit their new allies.

      * *

If this loyalist reaction is to be stopped

ANOTHER force that appeared upon the Irish scene was Irish syndicalism. Its socialist appeal was principally to the urban workers in Dublin and the other cities, but only marginally in Belfast. Its most famous leader—once James Larkin had departed to America after the great strike and lock-out of 1912–13—was James Connolly. He was a Marxist and undoubtedly the most important left-wing thinker and leader that modern Ireland has produced. Once in charge of the movement, the paper of which was *The Workers' Republic*, he proceeded to arm some two hundred of those workers, allegedly for self-protection against the police and military, ultimately for revolutionary purposes with intention an all-Irish Socialist Republic. His Citizen Army fought gallantly in 1916. He himself, having acted as a leader during that insurrection, was court-martialled by the British Army and shot. He became a legendary figure, particularly to the Left in Ireland. Though he had great personal admiration for Connolly, Eamon de Valera did not accept his Marxist views nor his vision of Ireland's future as a Socialist Republic. He was not, however, to be averse to a high degree of industrial and service nationalization within a mixed economy.

Pádraig Pearse after the conferring of his degree of Ll.B., 1903

YET another figure coming into prominence—though in his case more behind the scenes, within the secret councils of a revived and youthful I.R.B.—was Pádraig Pearse, the young barrister, poet and schoolmaster who was to lead the Easter Rising of 1916 and to be executed in consequence thereof. His views of Ireland's future, once the British had gone or been expelled, are hard to define. It would seem that his was a pure nationalism, largely uninfluenced by economic or other social theory. There is no question that at least until he obtained office in 1932 as Prime Minister (Taoiseach), de Valera regarded himself as Pearse's heir and preserved thereafter an immense respect for, and devotion to, the dead leader, which he repeatedly expressed.

De Valera (second from the left, centre row) in football clothes, c.1903 (top left)

De Valera, c.1904 (bottom left)

De Valera after the conferring of his degree, 1904 (above)

The earliest photograph of de Valera wearing glasses (below)

WITH these first stirrings of revolutionary activity, themselves well-nigh invisible in the Ireland that James Joyce was to immortalise in the amber of his *Ulysses*, the young de Valera had no contact, and until after the century's first decade had passed, he probably felt little interest in them, though he did join the Gaelic League in 1908.

The photographs opposite, which show him not only in football clothes but also in shooting attire, were taken at Rockwell in 1903 and 1904. In that year he obtained a pass, not an honours, degree in mathematics from the Royal University. He then achieved appointments at various schools, universities and teachers' training colleges in and about Dublin. At last, in 1912, he won a part-time temporary post as lecturer in mathematics and mathematical physics at Ireland's greatest and most famous seminary, St Patrick's College, Maynooth. This reinforced his already very considerable contact with the Roman Catholic priesthood, contacts which were to be of considerable importance and great support to him in the years to come.

Eamon and Sinéad de Valera after their wedding, 1910

De Valera teaching Irish at Tawin, Co. Galway, 1912

BY then he was married and a father. He had met Sinéad Ní Fhlannagáin (Flanagan) in 1908, when that attractive young woman was among the teachers from whom he was learning the Irish language. There was a summer school at Tourmakeady in the wild and beautiful, Gaelic-speaking area of the County Mayo, far from Dublin and the Home Rule and Ulster crisis that was to blow up in 1910. It was in those lovely surroundings that he courted and won his wife. Their initial shared interest was the Irish language in which both of them were soon fluent: indeed it has been said that during the sixty and more years of their marriage it was the language that they usually spoke in their home, to one another and to their eight children. They were married on 8 January 1910.

At first they had to live modestly on his pay as a teacher and this style of life they maintained, even when he became Prime Minister, President and indisputably the most famous of living Irishmen, a role he filled from 1917.

Save as his wife, Mrs de Valera did not take an active part in public life, though she knew exactly what was going on, particularly during the period called 'the Troubles'. Busy with her children and her home, she has been a model wife who never embarrassed her husband by airing political opinions that might not have always coincided with his own or, alternatively, that he might for tactical reasons wish to remain, at the time, unuttered. If his long absences, in America and in prison, grieved her and her children, she never complained, for she understood the inevitability of these.

F. E. Smith, M.P. (later Lord Birkenhead) speaking at an anti–Home Rule meeting, 1912

Ulster Volunteers drilling, Belfast, c.1912

THE new Irish crisis which began to boil up in 1910, the year of the de Valera marriage, was essentially of English party-political origin. The majority that the Liberals of H. H. Asquith (1852–1928) held over the Conservative opposition, was so small that he could only govern with the support of the Irish members. Redmond's price and that of the other Irish M.P.s was Home Rule, which had not interested the previous Liberal administration enjoying an overall majority from 1906 to 1910. And Home Rule meant a drastic constitutional curtailment to power in the House of Lords, an innovation which was not unacceptable to the Asquith government, though neither he nor his principal assistants, Grey, Winston Churchill and Lloyd George, were ever particularly enthusiastic about Home Rule as such.

The reaction in Ulster was quick and violent. Led by James Craig, later Lord Craigavon but then the leader of the Ulster M.P.s, by Edward Carson (1857–1935), a Dublin barrister, and by F. E. Smith (1872–1930), an Englishman later to be ennobled as Lord Birkenhead, they had the full, one might even say the ferocious, backing of the British Conservative and Unionist Party, of the Ulster Presbyterians ('Home rule means Rome rule'), of most army officers and of a very high proportion of the Protestant population, then as now some twenty percent in Ireland as a whole.

De Valera in 1910 was bitterly disappointed when he failed to win an appointment to the executive council of the Gaelic League. The Irish Republican Brotherhood, then engaged on a take-over of the League, saw to it that one of its own nominees was elected. De Valera does not then seem to have known that the I.R.B. even existed, and blamed Arthur Griffith's Sinn Féin, vowing that he would never have anything to do with it. However with Ireland headed for the crisis of Home Rule, and perhaps for bloodshed, he could clearly not remain detached from politics much longer.

Sir Edward Carson, first signatory of the Ulster Covenant, Belfast City Hall, 1912

IN an atmosphere of political hatred such as England has seldom known, the House of Lords Reform Bill was rammed through Parliament in 1911. Almost equally contentious was the next major item on the agenda, Home Rule, which the reformed House of Lords could now only delay for two years unless the United Kingdom government were meanwhile to fall.

In the autumn of 1912 most of the Protestant adult population of that province signed the Ulster Covenant, some in their own blood. They were thus dedicated to resist Home Rule by all means, including the use of force, and with this intention a body called the Ulster Volunteers, soon to be armed with guns bought in Germany and elsewhere, was created. One of the first men, perhaps *the* first, to sign the Covenant was Edward Carson.

British soldiers unloading coal at the Dublin docks, 1913

Irish Citizen Army parade outside Liberty Hall, Dublin, 1914

THE other provinces and religious persuasions of Ireland did not immediately respond to this provocation on the part of the Ulster Unionists, being, in the urban areas at least, deeply involved in a most violent strike and lock-out.

On the opposite page British soldiers are shown unloading a collier in the Port of Dublin in 1913, in defiance of the strike called by the Irish Transport and General Workers' Union. The strike and lock-out led to bloodshed and death.

Connolly's Citizen Army was the workers' response. It must be repeated that its creation was a syndicalist rather than a simple nationalist phenomenon. In the background of the photograph is Liberty Hall, the headquarters then as now (rebuilt after 1916 and again in the 1960's) of the Irish Transport and General Workers' Union.

Dr Eoin MacNeill and Thomas Kettle at the inaugural meeting of the Irish Volunteers, 25 November 1913

Irish Volunteers drilling early in 1914 before the importation of arms

THE mobilising and the arming of the Ulster Volunteers, and not less the sympathy that they evoked among British officers of the regular army, caused anxiety that was to lead to emotions approaching consternation in London's government circles. By then Home Rule, ticking away like a time-bomb, could not be delayed by the House of Lords beyond early 1915 if the new, normal constitutional procedures were to be observed. During that same fateful year Carson lunched with the German Kaiser and bought guns which were most skilfully run into Larne, Co. Antrim, and distributed among the Ulster Volunteers with a minimum of interference from the British authorities. Ulster's Protestants had now, in fact, an efficient, well-organised and quite well equipped army in being, to fight against Home Rule. Its leaders had good reason to believe that it would not be fighting against the British army—the only armed force that could defeat it—but against its largely unorganised and unarmed Roman Catholic compatriots in Ireland as a whole.

Therefore, and with a curious slowness, the Irish nationalists responded. A meeting was held at the Rotunda Rink, Dublin, on 25 November 1913, to enroll soldiers for a counterforce, the Irish Volunteers. Among the audience was Eamon de Valera, who was one of the first to enroll and was soon to assume officer rank. He has said that he could not hear Kettle, the chairman, for he was shouted down by workers who accused him of strike-breaking.

The I.R.B. largely controlled this new force but deliberately picked Professor MacNeill, the Gaelic scholar, as its titular head precisely because he was not a member of the Organisation, which indeed kept very much in the shadows, and was therefore less likely to frighten the British authorities than any man identified with themselves or Sinn Féin.

The now armed Motor Cycle Corps of the
Ulster Volunteers, Belfast, 1914 (top)

Mrs Erskine Childers and Mary Spring-Rice,
daughter of Lord Monteagle, on board the
Asgard while sailing down the English
Channel (above left)

Mary Spring-Rice and Erskine Childers
during the unloading of the Asgard (left)

Mrs Reddin leading a contingent of the
Cumann na mBan in the funeral of
Mr Pigeon, a victim of the Bachelor's Walk
shooting (above)

THE organisation of this, the third, private army to appear in Ireland in as many years was easier than the procurement of arms. Winston Churchill, now First Lord of the Admiralty, had sent large contingents of the Royal Navy to prevent a repetition of the Larne gun-running. Erskine Childers, an Irish patriot of English extraction, and Mary Spring-Rice, Irish daughter of the British Ambassador in Washington, ran in a number of single-shot rifles, bought in Germany, to Howth, aboard his own yacht, the *Asgard*.

This happened in the summer of 1914. The guns, some of which were intended for de Valera's command, were transferred into Dublin with far less skill than had been shown by the Ulstermen after the Larne gun-running. The military opened fire in Bachelor's Walk, Dublin and there were fatal casualties. This, combined with the apparent tolerance of the Larne gun-running, caused extreme anger among the Irish Volunteers. With the outbreak of the First World War, a few weeks later, the leaders of the I.R.B. decided upon an armed Irish rebellion at the earliest opportunity. One of the officers under their command, though not among the most senior, was Eamon de Valera, who held a rank equivalent to that of a battalion commander and who, at the time of the Bachelor's Walk incident and later, showed a brief but remarkable aptitude for the science of soldiering: for he always approached it, in at least this first instance, as a mathematician.

British Troops at the Curragh, 1914

THE so-called Mutiny at the Curragh (the main training area for the British army in Ireland) was an incident much exaggerated at the time—the summer of 1914—and by many historians since. Certain senior, and some very senior, officers told the United Kingdom Secretary of State for War that they would resign their commissions rather than see their soldiers used to disarm the Ulster Volunteers or even to prevent those irregulars stealing guns from British army stores. Asquith's government surrendered to this weird demand: no officers were cashiered, though the Secretary of State who had capitulated to them was dismissed.

It has been said, on almost no evidence, that this incident convinced the German government that the British army was contemptible. Events in the very near future were to prove precisely the contrary.

In Ireland, however, in the mounting emotions of 1914, 'the Curragh' was interpreted, and particularly by the I.R.B., as proof that Home Rule was a sham. With the outbreak of the First World War those men decided to enlist, if this were possible, German support for an Irish revolution. Sir Roger Casement was sent to Berlin, via New York, to arrange this.

With the outbreak of the World War, with the incorporation of the Ulster Volunteers into the 36th (Ulster) Division that was to be decimated in the Battle of the Somme (June 1916) and with Redmond's public pronouncement of nationalist Irish support for Britain in a war to 'liberate' Belgium, the 'Curragh Mutiny' became an almost irrelevant footnote to Anglo-Irish relations, though a gift to the rhetorical republican extremists.

Pádraig Pearse addressing a recruiting meeting for the Irish Volunteers near Dublin 1915 (above)

Pádraig Pearse, near top left, delivers his funeral oration at O'Donovan Rossa's grave, 1915 (centre)

Reviewing Irish Volunteers at Maryboro' (now Portlaoise) after the passage of the Home Rule Suspensory Act.
With cigar: John Redmond, M.P.
On his left, his son Captain Redmond

JOHN Redmond realised, rather belatedly in 1914, that the Volunteers were a potential political force which he therefore wished to control. The Citizen Army was of course beyond his grasp. A photograph opposite shows men of both organizations, with Pádraig Pearse, at the graveside of the old Fenian, O'Donovan Rossa in 1915. Among the officers in uniform who had marched in the cortège to Glasnevin cemetery was Eamon de Valera. By then, however, the Volunteers had split.

The I.R.B. leaders had not objected to Redmond's successful attempt to take over the Volunteers. It suited their policy to make the movement appear respectable in British eyes, while they kept the reality of power firmly in their own hands. However in August 1914, on the outbreak of the War, Redmond declared himself, his Irish Party and 'his' Volunteers as firmly loyal to the British cause. This split the movement, the Redmondites being henceforth known as the Nationalist Volunteers. Those theoretically commanded by MacNeill but in fact controlled by the I.R.B. were the Irish Volunteers.

For de Valera there was of course no choice. However he was becoming increasingly dissatisfied with what was virtually a system of dual command within the Irish Volunteers. Two men under his command, Seán Fitzgibbon and The O'Rahilly, were members of the I.R.B., which he was not, and therefore they had information and thus potential power denied to their commanding officer.

A solution was reached, whereby they were transferred to another command, while Eamon de Valera was sworn in by Thomas MacDonagh as a member of the I.R.B. However, de Valera, for reasons which are obscure but are perhaps of religious origin, was opposed to secret societies as such and told MacDonagh that he would attend no I.R.B. meetings. Nor did he. Henceforth, however, the plans of the I.R.B. were accessible to him.

Eamonn Ceannt, 1882–1916 (top)

Joseph Plunkett, 1887–1916 c. 1914 (centre)

Seán MacDermott, 1883–1916 c.1915 (left)

Thomas MacDonagh, 1878–1916 c.1915 (above)

FOUR of the I.R.B. leaders who were to organise the Easter Rising, fight in it after signing the Declaration of an Irish Republic, and to suffer death when it was defeated, are portrayed on the opposite page; Thomas MacDonagh (1878–1916), Joseph Plunkett (1887–1916), Seán MacDermott (1883–1916) and Eamonn Ceannt (1882–1916).

Much obscurity, inevitably, darkens the activities of the I.R.B. between 1914 and 1916. It would seem, however, probable that the most powerful men, the decision-makers, were MacDonagh, Plunkett, Casement, in America, Devoy, and only later, Pearse. De Valera was not of their number, and no more was Michael Collins who, though a member of the I.R.B., only returned from England to Ireland a few months before the Easter Rising. The Organisation's old leadership was destroyed, quite deliberately, by British firing squads in 1916. One reason why de Valera was spared his comrades' fate was that, not being an active member of the I.R.B., he had not signed the Proclamation of a Republic.

Commandant de Valera in Irish Volunteer's uniform, c.1915

De Valera's house in Greystones, Co. Wicklow, as it was 1971

DE VALERA was not only commander of the third battalion but also adjutant of the Dublin brigade, four battalions strong, commanded by Mac-Donagh. During this year, 1915, he studied military manuals intensively, as well as supervising the training of his men. On 13 March 1915, the plan for the uprising, then intended for the autumn of that year, was explained by Pádraig Pearse to the military and political leaders. Each battalion was to be responsible for the neutralisation of one British barracks in Dublin, the third battalion being assigned the Beggar's Bush Barracks, which meant in effect the area between Westland Row (Pearse) railway station and the Grand Canal. Its second, but perhaps more important mission would be the interdiction of the railway between Kingstown (now Dún Laoghaire) where British reinforcements would probably land, and Westland Row. De Valera repeatedly reconnoitred his future operational area, usually on foot and was frequently accompanied, for camouflage, by his small son. He took his responsibilities as a soldier and a commander very seriously indeed.

He and his family were now living at Greystones, then a small seaside dormitory suburb some fifteen miles south of Dublin, in a modest house. He therefore usually travelled to and from work on the railway line that passes through Dún Laoghaire. Since the Rising, originally planned for the autumn of 1915, was finally—in the following January—fixed for Easter, 1916, he thus had ample time both to study his terrain and to know and train his men.

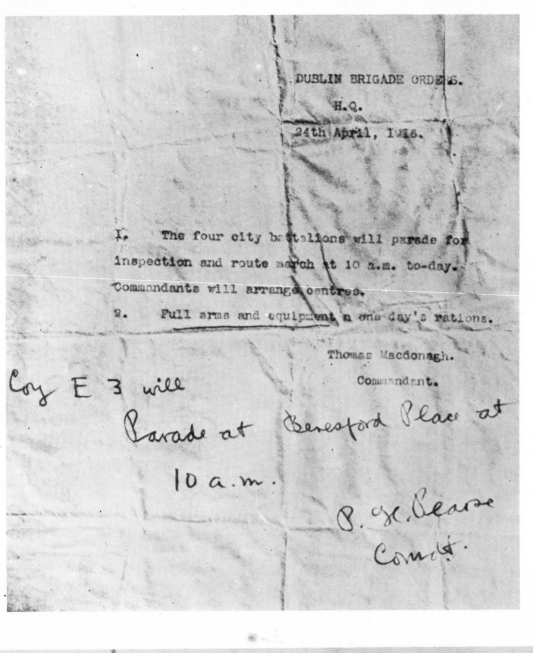

DUBLIN BRIGADE ORDERS.

H.Q.

24th April, 1916.

1. The four city battalions will parade for inspection and route march at 10 a.m. to-day. Commandants will arrange centres.

2. Full arms and equipment n one day's rations.

Thomas Macdonagh.

Commandant.

Coy E 3 will Parade at Beresford Place at 10 a.m.

P. H. Pearse
Comdt.

Mobilisation order, 1916, superseding MacNeill's cancellation of previous order

Boland's Bakery, H.Q. of de Valera's command, 1916

IT IS not intended here to describe yet again the Easter Rising. It began with the failure of Casement either to import German arms and arrange a German diversion or, desperately, in view of this double failure in Germany, to cancel the operation. Only a fraction, perhaps some 2,000 men, of the Volunteers assisted by some 250 of the Citizen Army obeyed Pearse's mobilisation order in defiance of MacNeill's order to call this off. The Irish, who had no artillery and almost no signals network, were soon outnumbered, at least 10 to 1, by a fully equipped and well trained British army. Nevertheless they fought for nearly a week, with very little support from the populace.

De Valera's third battalion, very much under strength owing to the mobilisation muddle, had as its principal strongpoint Boland's Bakery, on the Grand Canal, usually and incorrectly referred to as Boland's Mill. He and his men inflicted a tactical defeat on the British marching from Kingstown, nor did he surrender the big building until ordered to do so after the collapse of the Rising in other areas of Dublin.

He was never again to be a soldier on active service. This single week, however, had proved both his skill as a commander and his tenacity as a man.

*Commandant de Valera marches at the
head of his men after surrender,
Dublin 1916*

De Valera under prisoners' escort, 1916

TYPICALLY, he marched into captivity at the head of his men. He was never again to accept willingly any role other than that of a leader. Typical too, perhaps, is the exhausted defiance of his expression in the photograph opposite while being marched to court-martial after a sleepless week of bitter fighting and defeat.

One of the very few leaders to escape the firing squads of the British Army, he vanished for over a year into various English prisons. There he caused his gaolers the maximum trouble, insisting that he be treated with the dignity of a political prisoner and not as a felon.

By the time he was released, in the summer of 1917, the political climate both in Britain and Ireland had changed utterly. He returned as a hero and was immediately elected a Member of Parliament, as Sinn Féin candidate, for the East Clare constituency.

Sir Matthew Nathan, Under-Secretary, and Chief Secretary Augustine Birrell, Dublin, after the Rising

General Sir John Maxwell, c.1916

THE PENDULUM in Britain's attitude to Ireland was swinging ever more rapidly under the pressures of world war, revolution in Russia and the imperative necessity not to offend the United States with its powerful Irish-American lobby. In the nineteenth century that pendulum had swung between coercion and conciliation. In ours the words would be oppression and appeasement.

Dublin Castle, where the administration had been controlled in 1916 by Chief Secretary Augustine Birrell and Under-Secretary Sir Matthew Nathan, had believed that, in Balfour's words, they had 'killed Home Rule through kindness'. The Easter Rising blew them, and with them Redmond, parliamentarianism and appeasement out of existence. So oppression was tried. Martial Law was imposed under Sir John Maxwell who was instructed by H. H. Asquith and his government to crush the Irish rebels' leaders. These orders he obeyed quickly, ruthlessly and partly in secret. This, too, failed as a policy. The Irish people had been, in general, hostile to the men of the Rising. The executions began to rally them, finally almost in unanimity except in Ulster, behind Sinn Féin. Lloyd George, by then Asquith's successor as Prime Minister, decided therefore to try appeasement once again, though by the time de Valera returned to his own country nobody in London seriously intended that all Ulster would be included in some future Irish state. He came back in 1917 to a very different Ireland, to be greeted as a hero and accepted as a leader, one of the few important survivors of what was beginning to become, and has remained, an incident of traumatic importance in the history of the Irish people.

Irish National Convention, 1917, with Redmond, Mahaffy and George Russell

The return of Eamon de Valera to Ireland, 1917 (left)

De Valera hears of his election as a Sinn Féin T.D. at East Clare, 1917. He is in Irish Volunteer officer's uniform (below)

LLOYD GEORGE had released the Irish prisoners because he intended in 1917 to summon an all-Irish Convention to 'solve the Irish question' or at least to quieten the Irish-American lobby temporarily in the United States, until such time as America was fully committed to the war in Europe.

Boycotted by Sinn Féin (for whom de Valera had been elected as a Member of Parliament) and sabotaged by the Orangemen both in Ulster and in London, it was not only a non-starter as a conference but set the scene for the massive boycott by Sinn Féin of all British administration in Ireland, including the law courts and the collection of taxes. This was quite soon to make civilian rule in Ireland impossible. As an intrinsic part of Sinn Féin policy, de Valera never took his seat in the United Kingdom House of Commons, since he and the other Sinn Féin M.P.s regarded themselves as elected to a then non-existent, all-Irish parliament called Dáil Eireann.

In that same year, 1917, de Valera broke off his relations with the I.R.B. Later in that year, after a conversation in a Dublin restaurant off Grafton Street with Count Plunkett, father of the executed I.R.B. leader, and Arthur Griffith he agreed to be proposed as candidate as President of Sinn Féin to be elected democratically at the general Party meeting that November.

Englishmen and Irishmen, with any political acumen, were now realising that a revolutionary situation was in existence, and that a revolution was likely soon enough to become inevitable. In the Anglo-Irish War de Valera was to be cast, and ever more to cast himself, in the role of statesman, of Ireland's conscience and political leader. His days as a soldier on active service were over, and forever, before his fortieth birthday. Henceforth he was to cloak himself with a certain, deliberate remoteness against the turmoil. Such a withdrawal into dignity is more likely to inspire public respect than public affection.

Thomas Ashe, 1884–1917 c.1915

IN THE new climate of Irish political opinion new men were appearing to replace the dead leaders. They were to be younger, more ruthless and almost without the element of romanticism, of the gesture, which had inspired Pearse and some of his friends, inherited from Young Ireland long ago. They were preparing for war, brutal twentieth century war, in which victory *by any means* is the sole objective.

Apart from de Valera the only commandant who had fought in 1916 and had escaped the firing-squads was Thomas Ashe (1884–1917). A prisoner of the British, he went on hunger strike in 1917, was forcibly fed and died. The Irish equated his death with murder.

Liam Mellowes (1892–1922) was a socialist who inherited the mantle of James Connolly. He was to die at the hands of his compatriots, a hostage held and executed by the Free State forces in the Civil War.

Erskine Childers and his cousin Robert Barton were Protestant Anglo-Irishmen who for idealistic reasons had become utterly devoted to the cause of Irish freedom. Childers, too, was executed after an almost farcical trial during the Civil War. Barton (1881) one of the plenipotentaries sent to London in 1921 to arrange the Treaty, survived.

Field-Marshal Lord French conferring decorations in Dublin Castle, 1918

BUT THE man who was to become most famous, and ultimately the most legendary of the new generation of leaders was undoubtedly Michael Collins. A member of the I.R.B., he had fought at the General Post Office as a staff officer during the Rising. The British authorities had not recognised his importance and he was released, with many other apparently unimportant Irish prisoners, from the Welsh concentration camp in which they were incarcerated, late in 1916. (The more important prisoners, such as Eamon de Valera, were held in prisons, and not released for a further six months or so.) Before their release, indeed while he was still a prisoner in Wales, Collins had set about the reconstruction of the I.R.B.—of which he was soon to be leader—as a conspiratorial and military-political force, and soon enough as an economic entity too. He, more perhaps than anyone else, put together the pieces smashed in 1916. 'The Big Fellow' did not aspire for personal prominence and, at least until 1921, loyally and, it would seem totally, accepted the leadership of de Valera as the President of Sinn Féin and later of the embryonic Irish Republic. Brave and clever, modestly loyal for he was himself able to command the utmost loyalty, this great man of action, to quote President de Valera's own words to this writer in 1968, was one of Ireland's true heroes.

Anti-conscription oath being taken in Dublin, 1918

THE YEAR 1918 was, for Ireland, the eye of the hurricane, as the violent emotion of 1916 and 1917 subsided for some, while others, Irish and Englishmen alike, were well aware that there was even greater violence to come. The Americans were, by March 1918, fully committed to the Great War which the Central Powers still then believed that they could win. In Ireland, though almost all the patriots were at liberty and were consolidating their strength, Sinn Féin was no longer automatically winning every bye-election. David Lloyd George was then Prime Minister of a government which, theoretically, was a Coalition but which, so far as Irish matters were concerned, was essentially Unionist, for it included Carson, Smith and Winston Churchill who was thankfully ridding himself of his quite brief Liberal allegiance in order to revert to the policies of his imperialist father.

In Britain the pendulum was swinging again, in 1918, once the Irish Convention had failed to find any solution to problems intractable within the British Empire and the United Kingdom of the time. In the spring of 1918 Lloyd George's government decided to implement conscription in Ireland, to replace dead soldiers in France and the Low Countries. In Ireland itself there were massive counter-demonstrations. Why should Irish manhood be compelled to die for Ireland's conquerors? The authorities in London stupidly responded with the arrest of de Valera; and many more of the leaders of Sinn Féin, in May of 1918. He was to be a prisoner again, on no real charge, for over six months. Among the few Irish leaders who escaped the net was Michael Collins, on whom great responsibility therefore devolved.

PART TWO

IN IRELAND too, a national war distorts political issues and, for its duration, political philosophy and even personality can become subservient to efficiency and force. Famous faces disappear, others emerge with startling clarity, while some are transmuted by a new light: in 1940, Neville Chamberlain, Charles de Gaulle, Winston Churchill. In Ireland, during the tragedies and triumphs of 1917 to 1923 and later, a period when, in Yeats' phrase, 'all changed, changed utterly', the figure of Eamon de Valera was also transmogrified, at least in the eyes of others, though there is little evidence that either his inflexible character or his clear, sometimes chilly mathematician's eye, or indeed his apparently proud appraisal of the role assigned him both as man and as symbol in the unfolding destiny of his country, was modified by the events of those terrible years.

This is not the place, nor is there here the time, to deal in any but the briefest terms with the intensely complex events of that period. The political scene, both national and international, in Ireland (North and South), in Britain and in the United States was in flux, more so even than is 'normal'. (No other country was remotely interested in Irish affairs once Germany was defeated and the new Russian Communist leaders had seen that there was precious little soup for them to make out of Irish bones: though future nationalists in other reluctant areas of the British Empire watched Irish events with interest and sympathy.)

In Ireland, power was to pass from the hands of the politicians to the soldiers, British and Irish. Already by 1917 Redmond's parliamentary party was dying. Sinn Féin became a national liberation movement, above party politics. As a political party it rapidly followed Redmond's Irish Party into a sort of limbo for there was no opposition within Dáil Eireann until the Treaty of 1922. The I.R.B., led by Collins and others, assumed power, particularly after the outbreak of the Anglo-Irish War which it is usually agreed began in January of 1919. However a secret society can scarcely act as a government and, as the Second World War was to show, unless it has a firm backbone of economic and political ideology, such as in Tito's Yugoslavia, will disintegrate with victory to become either a new tyranny or to bleed itself to death in civil war: this was to happen in parts of

Dublin Metropolitan Police outside the Mansion House during the inaugural session of the first Dáil

France and Italy in 1945 and had already taken place in the new Irish Free State of 1922. By then, despite the immense efforts and energy of its leaders, the I.R.B. was itself close to death, for in the pressures and mounting brutalities of the Anglo-Irish War the central organisation of 'the Irish resistance' had become increasingly isolated from its men. The power of the gun thus passed from the soldiers and their officers to local guerrilla leaders and thence to gunmen.

On the British side, while Lloyd George's government continued to swing the pendulum, with an ever more violent motion, between oppression and appeasement, civilian government in Dublin was rapidly destroyed by the English and Irish alike. Indeed it never really recovered from 1916 and Maxwell's executions: it became an easy target for the policies of Sinn Féin and, later, for the assaults of armed men who quite quickly neutralised

Seán T. O'Kelly, T.D. and Gavan Duffy, T.D., the Irish delegates to Versailles (left)

Clemenceau, Wilson and Lloyd George at Versailles, 1919 (below)

The Irish Republican Army in training, 1919

Royal Irish Constabulary station destroyed by the Irish Republican Army, 1919

and then destroyed the Royal Irish Constabulary. The British military took over; but with the importation of new men, the so-called Black-and-Tans, to replace the now almost non-existent Irish police force, and the Auxiliaries who filled a somewhat more sinister role involving both intelligence and reprisals, British power, too, passed in large measure from the centre where decisions should be made to the periphery where they are carried out—from the generals and the staff officers, to the mercenary local commander and the gunman. This slide into anarchy was perhaps less pronounced, for obvious reasons, among the British than the Irish, but sufficiently so to arouse decent British public opinion against the activities of men in British uniforms

morality on Irish soil: his name was Oswald Mosley.

The Irish hoped for justice and freedom from Britain, but did not expect it. They expected it from America, particularly at the time of the Versailles peace conference, but did not get it, though from the Irish-Americans they received a great deal of moral support and much treasure. However, so long as the war was going on, the United States government regarded rebellion in Ireland as an anti-Allied, which also meant an anti-American, activity: and almost as soon as that war was won the headlong retreat into isolationism meant the isolation of President Woodrow Wilson and the reluctance of his, and his successors', governments to burn their fingers with foreign hot potatoes.

Eamon de Valera, perhaps in part because America was the country of his birth but more through his prestige, had been chosen as the Irish emissary to the United States during this time of trouble. Politically he failed, in a Washington where perhaps no Irishman could have succeeded: economically he was far more successful, and raised, by the sale of Irish Republican Bonds (redeemable when Ireland was free, and then speedily repaid)

Mrs. Wheelwright, de Valera's mother, at the time of his visit to her in 1919 (above)

British Troops detrain at Kingsbridge, Dublin. The train crew had refused to operate, 1919 (below)

against the Irish, and in that British public's name. This was a factor which the Lloyd George government could not indefinitely ignore in its adjustment of the pendulum's swing. The nascent Labour Party, being anticolonialist and in part pacifist, was strongly opposed to Lloyd George's policy in Ireland. The youngest English Conservative M.P. of the time, an ex-officer with a gallant record, crossed the floor to join them, disgusted by these insults to English

De Valera on tour in the United States,
1919 (above)

Michael Collins seated at the block on which
Robert Emmet was quartered, opens the
subscription for the Dáil Eireann first
internal loan, 1919 (right)

A meeting of a Dáil Eireann Commission,
illegal from the British point of view and
therefore secret, at the Mansion House,
Dublin, in December 1919 (below)

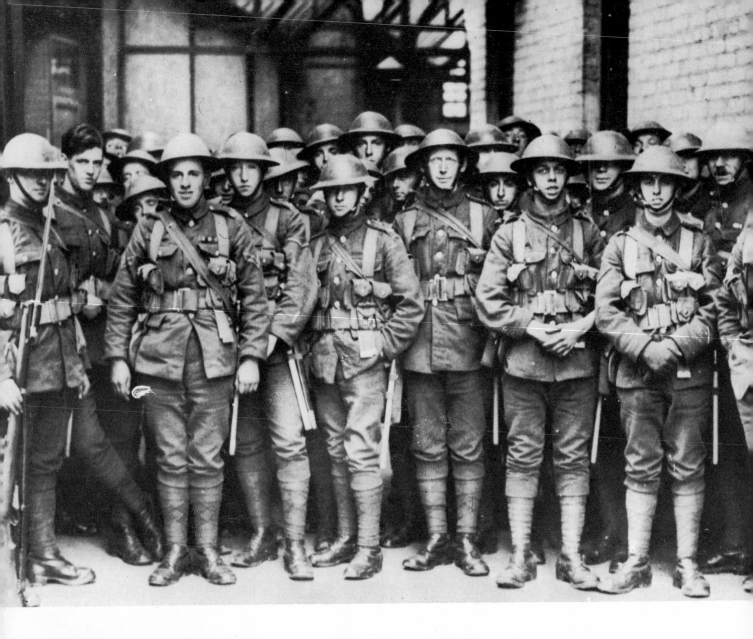

British troops occupy the Royal Irish Automobile Club after Dublin had been placed under martial law, December 1919

De Valera with Harry Boland in New York, 1920

several million dollars, the sinews of Irish resistance: in what would now be called the public relations sphere, his success was immense, as he travelled back and forth across the United States making impassioned speeches for the Irish cause. This very success, however, may have been something of a boomerang. No great power, and certainly not the United States of 1920, appreciates the spectacle of a politician from abroad mobilising a powerful minority in the interest of his own, small, distant country. Furthermore he also exported his own dislike of the I.R.B., which he did not conceal, and as a

result quarrelled quite bitterly with the most important figure on the Irish-American scene, that veteran Fenian, John Devoy.

De Valera was seldom an entirely free agent during the period here under discussion. Arrested again in May of 1918 he was 'sprung' from Lincoln Gaol by Michael Collins and Harry Boland, in person, and brought back secretly to Dublin in February of 1919, that is to say within weeks of the first shots being fired in the Anglo-Irish war. He left almost immediately for America, where he remained until his return to Ireland, again in secret, in December of 1920. By then almost all the Irish leaders were 'on the run' from the British agents.

De Valera at Butte, Montana, 1920 (above)

The Sinn Féin Bank after being raided by British troops, January 1920 (right)

British Lancia armoured car, Ireland,
1920 (right)

Auxiliaries surround the coffin of Terence
MacSwiney, who died in London,
arriving at Cork on board the tug
Mary Tavy, 1920 (below)

During his period of nearly two years in America he had, of course, been in frequent touch with the leaders in Ireland. Since, rapidly, neither the posts nor the telegraph could be used as a means of communication a fairly efficient courier service, using Irish seamen on the transatlantic route, was established. This was inevitably slow. In a war situation critical decisions have to be taken very quickly, and often there was not time to await the President's views before decisions, even decisions of major policy, were made in Dublin: though it seems that every attempt was made to give the President, certainly in word and possibly in deed, ultimate authority. A touching, personal example of this loyalty was provided by Collins who himself delivered messages and letters to Mrs de Valera, still then living with the children in the Greystones house, and this when he was being actively hunted by the British, a price that eventually reached £10,000 on his head dead

De Valera in the U.S.A., 1920 (left)

De Valera in California, 1920 (below)

Irish-American reaction to events in Ireland (above)

De Valera in the U.S.A., 1920, near the end of his American tour (right)

or alive, and the de Valera home one of the most dangerous houses he could visit. Nor, it would seem, could the absent President be kept fully informed of the rift that even before his return was beginning to divide the leaders in Ireland. This was, during the Anglo-Irish War, caused less by divergence of political views, for all were united in their determination to throw off British rule, but rather by the question of authority: and that, in turn, stemmed from the old question, which had vexed de Valera even before 1916, of the role of the I.R.B. Who was in charge, the ministers of a state still struggling to be born, usually invisible—apart from their very visible President far away in the United States—except when

Commandant Tom Barry, organiser of the Crossbarry operation (above)

Two Royal Irish Constabulary men in a street in Rathluirc (Charleville), 1921, where de Valera had been a schoolboy some 30 years before (below)

arrested and imprisoned by the enemy? Or the equally invisible, but more competently organised, leaders of the secret Brotherhood? Both organisations of course overlapped but the secrecy of the I.R.B. gave it a greater strength and its traditions, perhaps, a greater ruthlessness. As the war developed, its quality changed, for it became increasingly, and at last almost entirely, a war between the British and the Irish intelligence services. The one had the backing of vast experience and technical expertise: the other the strength

that it was operating in its own country with the support of the ovetwhelming majority of the Irish population, excluding elements of certain classes in all Ireland and the Protestants of all classes in parts of Ulster. This development is normal in a guerrilla or resistance situation. It had been proved in 1916 that the Irish could not, then and probably never, win a pitched battle against the armed forces of the British. On the other hand, they could *blind* these forces, a traditional Irish tactic. The destruction of the Royal Irish Constabulary was merely the first step, for when this had been achieved the Irish Director of Intelligence, Michael Collins, found his organisation confronted by the whole strength of British intelligence.

The word 'intelligence' bears an implication of intellectual, even scholarly, activity and, perhaps, quiet and gentlemanly crime: the breaking of codes and cyphers, the tapping of telephones, the stealing of mail, the planting of false information, eaves dropping at dinner parties and the evaluation of espionage reports generally. All this happens, and happened in Ireland, but the reality, in a guerrilla situation, is far more brutal. It involves no less than the physical destruction of the enemy's intelligence officers, unless these can be bought (which is rare) and by any methods: it means the destruction of men even suspected as informers: it can, and on occasion in Ireland did, mean the use of torture to extract vital information from prisoners. That was the basis on which the Anglo-Irish War was being fought, by both sides, when President de Valera returned from America in December of 1920. The casualties were remarkably light, the war climate atrocious, and nerves close to breaking point. When he arrived back he believed, incorrectly it would seem, that the British authorities wished to re-arrest him, and until May of 1921 he lived more or less in hiding. Had the British in fact wished to pick him up it would seem incredible that they should have failed to do so, and this for numerous reasons. The first and simplest was physical. Whereas Michael Collins, whom the British certainly had wished to arrest, was unphotographed for many years, de Valera's face was known from a thousand pictures in the American press and earlier. Collins looked very much 'the ordinary Irishman', a big one

De Valera at the time of the Truce,
1921

Óglaiġ na h-Éireann.

Áro-Oiṗiġ, áṫ Cliaṫ.   General Headquarters, Dublin.

Department...............
Reference No................

9th. July, 1921.

TO:
Officers Commanding All Units.

In view of the conversations now being entered into by our Government with the Government of Great Britain, and in pursuance of mutual understandings to suspend hostilities during these conversations, active operations by our troops will be suspended as from Noon Monday July, Eleventh.

C/S.

British troops searching among the
remnants of the destroyed taxation records in
the Custom House, Dublin, 1921

British troops at Carrick-on-Suir, 1921 (left)

Thomas Whelan and Patrick Moran accompanied by an Auxiliary R.I.C. in Mountjoy Gaol, 13 March 1921. They had been convicted after an equivocal identification and were executed by hanging on the following day (below)

in a country where big men abound, able to melt into a crowd. De Valera's very tall, thin body and his gaunt, perhaps even Iberian, features made him almost unique. It would seem unlikely that even the most stupid policeman or secret agent could, from then to the day of his death, have failed to recognise him. Furthermore he was only in semi-hiding. Though he avoided public appearances and changed house, he resumed living with his family and was picking up the reins of his presidential authority, which meant repeated meetings, at his home or even elsewhere, with other, theoretically 'wanted', men whom in the circumstances it would not have been so difficult to trace. Finally it may be assumed that as the British pendulum, under the pressure of public opinion, swung back towards appeasement of the Irish, this world-famous man would have been a most awkward, indeed unwelcome, prisoner. It would thus seem probable that when he was arrested and thrown into gaol, on 18 May 1921, this was a British administrative error perfectly comprehensible in the chaotic circumstances, with the multiple chains of overlapping command then prevailing in Ireland. Or it may have been one of Lloyd George's cat-and-mouse tricks, for he was released five weeks later. By then a letter was on the way from the Prime Minister of the United Kingdom to the recognised Irish

The men who signed the Treaty. Left to right: T.D.s Griffith, Duggan, Barton and Gavan Duffy (Michael Collins travelled separately)

Winston Churchill, M.P., P.C., and General Nevil Macready, Inverness Conference, September 1921

First Irish delegation to London, 12 July 1921. L to R: R. C. Barton, Eamon de Valera, Count Plunkett, Arthur Griffith, Erskine Childers

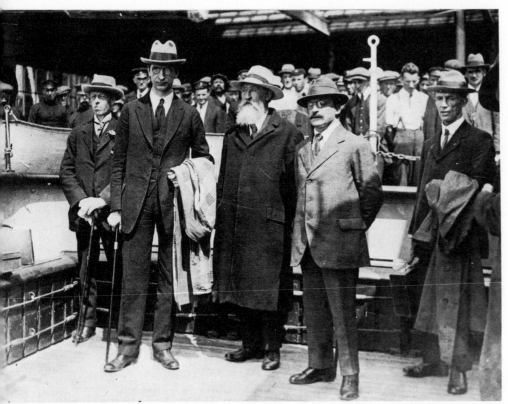

leader requesting an immediate conference for the purpose of arranging a truce. By then much had happened of great importance to Ireland's history but with which Eamon de Valera, because of being technically in hiding, was seldom directly involved. The first Dáil had met, elected ministers, most of whom attended its debates although under its proscription later in that year they were liable to arrest on sight: the Government of Ireland, 1920, Act was on the United Kingdom statute book, so that Britain was pledged by law to the preservation of Protestant Ulster, at least, and all Ulster, at most, within the United Kingdom: there had been violent anti-Catholic riots, a virtual pogrom, in Belfast and elsewhere in the North: and the I.R.A., though still active, was running desperately short of arms, ammunition and money. In the military sense, therefore, and in the political sense so far as Ulster was concerned, Lloyd George's offer of a truce was made from a position of very great strength. Otherwise he would hardly have made it. From a moral, and therefore from another political, point of view, both in Ireland and in Britain, he was in a position of weakness and this was realised not only by himself and his Cabinet but also by his monarch and, we may safely

De Valera and Cathal Brugha take the salute at a review of the Western Division of the Irish Republican Army, December, 1921, at the time of the final negotiations in London

Robert Barton, T.D., 1881–

The Prime Minister, David Lloyd George, King George V, Lord Birkenhead (F. E. Smith) after signing of the Articles of Agreement for a Treaty, 6 December 1921

assume, by Eamon de Valera. Otherwise the Irishman would hardly have accepted this personal confrontation with the enemy. When he went to England, with almost no diplomatic training, it was to face conferences with one of the shrewdest, and, it must be said, most unscrupulous politicians that even the long history of Great Britain has ever produced.

It was, from all accounts, an agonising business. De Valera, it seems, talked from the mystical basis of Irish history, Lloyd George from the basis of *Realpolitik,* fields which each of them knew well but which have little in common. (When Lloyd George's grumble that discussion with de Valera was comparable to an attempt to pick up mercury with a fork was reported to him, de Valera is said to have replied: 'Why did he not try a spoon?') A truce was agreed, the shooting stopped, and the British government demanded an immediate conference to sign a treaty

De Valera after his election to the Chancellorship of the National University of Ireland, December 1921

De Valera and some of the Republican T.Ds. who left the Chamber after the vote in favour of the acceptance of the Articles of Agreement, 1922

between a partitioned Ireland and a United Kingdom which by now included the province of Ulster. It is marvellous when war, bloodshed and murder cease. Most people in England and Ireland felt this. But the bone of Ulster was now in the Irish throat, and therefore some Irishmen felt otherwise. The most prominent of these was Eamon de Valera, though some of the generals in the Irish Republican Army had, even in their state of military impoverishment, greater means at their disposal to right what he and they regarded as a wrong.

The second half of 1921, which saw the liquidation of the Anglo-Irish War, the consequent split within Sinn Féin, and then the rapid slide towards civil war, was a period of intense political activity in Ireland generally and for Eamon de Valera, now functioning openly as leader of the *de facto* Irish government, in particular. Although Sinn Féin had in effect already taken over the civil government of Ireland, there was a mass of administrative innovation against the day when it would be the *de jure* government as well.

This was one reason why he decided he must remain in Dublin and not personally take part in the Treaty negotiations in London. He therefore sent a delegation to London led by Collins and Griffith with plenipotentiary powers subject to ratification of all major decisions by de Valera's cabinet. (Nobody at the time seems to have attached enough importance to the inherent ambiguity of the Irish delegates' instruction, for a man is

Austin Stack, T.D., 1880–1929 (top left)

Cathal Brugha, T.D., 1874–1922 (top centre)

Michael Collins, at the meeting in 1922 required by the Treaty of the Parliament of Southern Ireland elected under the Government of Ireland Act, 1920. (top right)

Arthur Griffith, also at the meeting of the 'Parliament of Southern Ireland' (middle)

De Valera opens the anti-Treaty campaign, Dublin, 1922 (below)

The election 'pact' meeting, 1922.
Left to right: Harry Boland, Michael
Collins, Eamon de Valera, Arthur
Griffith, Countess Markievicz

Rory O'Connor, 1883–1922 (above)

De Valera speaking on behalf of the
Republican (Sinn Féin) party during
the 'pact' election campaign, June 1922
(right)

Civil War begins. Free State troops fire on the Republican soldiers in the Four Courts, Dublin, 28 June 1922

either a plenipotentiary or he is not. And who decides which decisions are major, which not? From this ambiguity immense harm was to result.) A second reason was, in his own words, his wish not to jeopardise the symbolic value of his Presidency by personally engaging in the inevitable deals and compromises that such a conference must and did entail. Collins, the soldier and I.R.B. leader, and Griffith, the political theorist and statesman, had far more freedom of manoeuvre. A third consideration may have been an awareness, after the Truce negotiations, that he was not the best man to deal with Lloyd George and the very formidable British team he brought to the conference.

Understandable as his reasons may have been, many have blamed him for his abstention from the Treaty negotiations. A Parnell, an O'Connell, a Tone would hardly have regarded himself as cast to play so Olympian a role during the very birth pangs of a new Irish state. He has been blamed even more for his refusal immediately to accept the terms at last agreed to and signed by the Irish pleni-potentiaries under the heaviest pressure,

amounting to an ultimatum from the British. This immediately split the Irish nationalist movement and led, within months, to civil war. Eamon de Valera's enemies have frequently blamed him for the civil war itself, but this is both partisan and unfair. He certainly did not desire a civil war, nor did he instigate it, nor even play any very prominent part in it, save in his efforts to end it.

There were three major points in the terms of the Treaty to which he objected. The one he disliked most strongly at the time was retention of British sovereignty in Ireland, which meant that the British monarch remained, in theory, the Irish Head of State represented by a Governor-General in Dublin. Collins saw this arrangement as ephemeral, transitory, and of no real or lasting importance. However for several years de Valera and his republican followers refused to take the oath of loyalty to the Crown, without which they could not take their seats in the Dáil. This tactic, reminiscent in different terms of O'Connell's before Catholic Emancipation, had a great emotional appeal to many Irishmen, though the pragmatists generally dis-

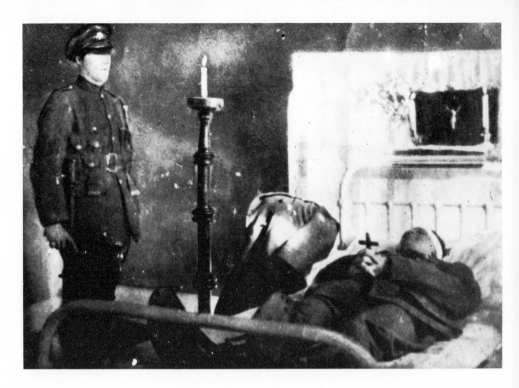

Michael Collins, the day of his death, Cork, 1922

Free State troops and guns being transported from Dublin by the mail boat, S.S. Cambria, *to Co. Cork, 1922 (below)*

Liam Lynch, 1890-1923

missed it. For them, any measure of self-government was better than none, for more must follow: *c'est le premier pas qui coûte.*

Secondly, he objected to those clauses in the Treaty which entitled the British to retain certain naval bases in the new Free State, the so-called Treaty Ports. This retention of practical, as well as theoretical, sovereignty in any part of Ireland was anathema to his, at that time almost abstract, patriotism. For simple

geographical and economic purposes, he was prepared to accept a measure of co-operation with Britain, but only as between two sovereign states. His phrase for this was 'external association with the British Empire', and his visual metaphor was that of the geometrician. Two circles may have contiguous circumferences, but the smaller circle can be either inside or outside the larger. He, of course, desired the second, nor did he ever change his mind. As late as 1969 this

writer saw the President of the Irish Republic draw his little diagram for the benefit of a visiting Cabinet Minister of the United Kingdom Government. A change of mind was never one of de Valera's habits: it was not until 1927, and with complicated semantic reservations, that he agreed to the oath and thus, with his followers of his new political party, took his seat in the Dáil.

The third, and at the time of writing still unresolved, Treaty issue was Partition. To this de Valera attached great importance, but less than many of the soldiers of the I.R.A. They wished immediately to invade the newly created and anomalous state, province or British protectorate known as Northern Ireland. The Irish government, of which de Valera was no longer a member after the Dáil had, by a small majority vote in January of 1922, ratified the Treaty which created the Irish Free State, knew that an invasion

Erskine Childers, 1870–1922

The office of the headquarters of the Republican Party, 20 December 1922 (below)

Railway bridge wrecked by Republican forces, 1923

Liam Mellowes, 1892–1922 (below)

Demonstration by Republican women, early 1923 (below right)

of the North by Republican extremist soldiers could only result in massive British military retaliation, which would almost certainly lead to the ruination if not the total destruction of the Free State.

On 13 April 1922, men of the Republican Army Executive, lead by Generals Rory O'Connor and Liam Lynch, seized the Four Courts in Dublin and repudiated all political allegiances. It was their intention to set up a military dictatorship with objective the conquest of Northern Ireland. Of the soldier-politicians involved in this the most prominent were Cathal Brugha, who had been Defence Minister, Liam Mellowes, the Socialist, and Erskine Childers. De Valera was not

De Valera with Joseph Creagh of Limerick, the day before the Ennis election meeting, 1923. Note that he has grown a beard as a disguise

of their number. Their opponents who were prepared, with British help, to break this attempt at a military *coup d'état* were led by their old comrades, Collins, Griffith, Kevin O'Higgins and W. T. Cosgrave, later President of the Executive Council. The result was a most brutal civil war that lasted for a year and saw the death of most of the leaders on both sides. The two most prominent survivors were Eamon de Valera and W. T. Cosgrave.

With Sinn Féin split and a general election pending, early in March of 1922 Eamon

De Valera addressing the election meeting. (He had shaved during the night)

de Valera and his principal lieutenants, Stack, Brugha and Mary MacSwiney had created a new, republican political party, Cumann na Poblachta. Within a few days the Republican officers led by Rory O'Connor defied a government ban on the holding of a military convention, repudiated the authority of the Dáil, and proceeded to seize the Four Courts. The officers did not consult with de Valera nor, it would seem, was he privy to their plans for sending men and munitions to the North though these were common knowledge in Dublin, Belfast and London. Under heavy pressure from London, the Irish government's forces were at last persuaded to attack the mutinous troops in the Four Courts on 28 July 1922.

The civil war had begun. De Valera had expressed his support for the Republican officers, but was himself passing through a period of political nausea. He re-enlisted, as a private, in his old battalion, the third, apparently in an attempt to escape the dilemma of his position. He was never a military leader in the civil war, and though his immense prestige made him a symbol of great value to the Republicans, the Irregulars as they were now called, their generals did not pay much heed to his council even when attempts were made to form a rival 'government' with himself at its head: indeed had they done so in early 1922 it is safe to say that there would have been no civil war or, later, that the squalid tragedy of treachery and atrocities would not have ended sooner. Nor is there any evidence that he was in any way connected with the death, in ambush, of Michael Collins in August, though he was in the vicinity at the time. (It is, however, possible that he was trying to meet Collins in order to find a formula that would end the fratricide.)

By late 1922 it was obvious that the Free State army would soon defeat the Irregulars and de Valera was attempting to negotiate with the government in Dublin headed by W. T. Cosgrave, with General Richard Mulcahy in control of military operations. He failed to secure terms better than the 'unconditional surrender' formula, which is hardly surprising for there is really no other way of ending a civil war save exhaustion and desertion. By the spring of 1923 the fighting was virtually over, though some two thousand Republicans were 'on the run',

Break up of Sinn Féin meeting, Ennis, Co. Clare, after de Valera's arrest, 1923. Crowds run from shooting

Eamon de Valera and, on his left, Austin Stack, as prisoners in Arbour Hill barracks, 1924

including de Valera. The government, however, felt sufficiently secure to hold a general election in August. De Valera decided to stand for Ennis, Co. Clare. While addressing an open air political meeting in that town on 15 August 1923, he was shot in the leg by Free State troops, arrested, and put in Arbour Hill prison. He thus once again found himself an imprisoned member of a parliament—for he had won the election by a 2 : 1 majority —but this time it was an Irish parliament and Irish gaolers. He was held, without trial, for nearly a year and was released on 16 July 1924. He spent his time in prison reading mathematics, playing chess and, no doubt, considering his own political future.

When on that summer's day of 1924 he emerged from prison into an exhausted, embittered, divided, impoverished Ireland, governed quite harshly by men whose political allegiance stretched from ex-Unionism to moderate Republicanism, Eamon de Valera had devoted eight years of his life almost exclusively to the political struggle, apparently to no avail, and most of those years had been spent far from his family and his own private interests, in prison, in America, in hiding. Yet he does not seem then, as he had done in early 1922, to have considered retirement from public life. Almost at once, from his home south of Dublin, he set about rebuilding the Republican base, from which he must operate, and the Republican image, which he must symbolise. What were to prove the most fruitful of his long years of service to his country, and to his own vision of how that country should develop, lay ahead.

PART THREE

A Royal Ulster Constabulary armoured car on the Border when de Valera was deported from his own constituency in Northern Ireland, 24 October 1924

HE WAS to be arrested once more, again by Irishmen but of a different sort.

He had been elected a member of the Northern Ireland parliament for a constituency in Co. Down, though he had of course never taken his seat at Stormont. With a general election pending in the North, he decided to visit his constituents, despite an order issued by the Northern Irish government that forbad him entry to any of the Six Counties save Co. Antrim, inaccessible except via Scotland. For sound political reasons he ignored this ban, crossed the Border on 24 October 1924, and was arrested in his own constituency at Newry. On the following day he was deposited by the Ulster authorities, using armoured cars, on the southern side of the Border. Four days later he was back in the North, in Derry via Co. Sligo. Charged with disobeying an order the validity of which he refused to recognise, in a court whose legality he likewise denied, he served a month's sentence in solitary confinement in a Belfast prison, with the harshest treatment he had ever experienced in any of the many prisons he had known.

His gesture did not affect the Partition issue, but it did rally support for the new political party that he was creating in the Free State, with himself as leader.

The formation of Fianna Fáil, Dublin, early 1926

THROUGHOUT 1925 de Valera was consolidating his position as the leader of those forces in Irish politics which had rejected the Treaty. By March of that year there were forty-eight deputies to the Dáil who refused to take the oath and thus debarred themselves from legislative activity. They still called themselves Sinn Féin, but that label had been rendered almost meaningless by the Civil War.

Early in 1926 his new party was officially founded at a meeting in Dublin. Named Fianna Fáil, which has been translated as 'the Warriors of Destiny', it took this somewhat bombastic name, hardly characteristic of de Valera's normal style, from Irish history almost as ancient as Ireland itself yet as modern as the events of 1916.

It claimed the heritage of Pádraig Pearse, and it was the executed leader's mother, who opened its newspaper, *The Irish Press,* some five years later on 5 September 1931. By then it had become a republican, but not a revolutionary, political party.

Cumann na nGaedheal, the anti-Fianna Fáil party, election posters, 1933

IN 1926, and indeed for many years to come, even perhaps until today, the *leit-motiv* of Irish politics, and particularly of internal Irish party-politics, was nationalism and the interpretation of Ireland's best interests in a political struggle that had led to bloody civil war between two sets of patriots. Cosgrave's future Fine Gael party was, in the nationalist sense, more gradualist than de Valera's Fianna Fáil. Both however were in economic and social matters essentially conservative and democratic. Their mutual animosity was rooted in history, expressed in personal hatred and almost entirely divorced from class or religious issues.

De Valera, as a political leader, was always a democrat, though at times a firm upholder of his beliefs. In 1926, and again for nationalist reasons, the army chiefs were contemplating a military government, General Mulcahy was then Defence Minister. General O'Duffy was in due course to create the Blueshirts, a fascist-type movement. De Valera steadfastly refused to accept such allies in his renewed struggle for an all-Irish Republic.

Eamon de Valera when first Taoiseach, with members of his first Fianna Fáil Cabinet, 1932

Fianna Fáil election posters, 1934

IN 1932 at a general election Fianna Fáil was for the first time returned to office with a small majority which was increased at another election two years later.

With the world economy in a most parlous condition as the depression deepened, economic problems were of primary importance. It seemed to the Irish highly unfair that the British government, by the terms of the Treaty, should continue to extract treasure from its ex-Colony. The so-called Tariff War with Britain resulted. Though it may be doubted whether this did the Irish economy, and therefore the Irish citizens, much good, it was certainly an acceptable tactic to the Irish whom the new government represented. Like other nation-states in Europe, Ireland decided to be self-supporting, to be an autarchy. In this effort, which involved considerable economic replanning on a national scale, Eamon de Valera had a most competent cabinet colleague in Seán Lemass, who was in due course to succeed him both as the leader of Fianna Fáil and as Taoiseach.

De Valera after being returned with a greatly increased majority for Fianna Fáil in the General Election of 1934

Blueshirts at Bluebell Cemetry, Dublin, 1934

THERE were other forces, political and social, which Eamon de Valera had to take into account in internal Irish affairs during his long years as leader of Fianna Fáil and, after 1932, as head of the government almost consistently until his election to the Presidency of the Republic in 1959.

The most extreme Republicans, whose leaders were released in 1932, frequently recruited for the new, and now illegal, Irish Republican Army. Their motive was the overthrow of British rule in Northern Ireland: their method, physical force and variants of terrorism. While agreeing with their objective, de Valera deplored and doubtless despised their means and was to treat them very roughly during the crisis of the Second World War. Another extremist force was the Blueshirts.

The small Irish Labour Party claimed the mantle of James Connolly and had, in some measure, the backing of the rather politically ineffective Irish trade unions. It was, however, subject to schism, in a country where class and materialism were not then the dominant factors that they were becoming in most of the western world.

For the masses the Church was still the most important teacher. The hierarchy was traditionally anti-Socialist, in part because of the inherent anti-clericalism, and indeed in the eyes of many clerics of this period ultimately atheistical, nature of the Socialist ideology. De Valera, though an extremely devout Christian, knew from personal experience how dangerous a political animal is a political priest. During the Civil War the hierarchy had ordered that the rites of the Church be refused to Republicans. He believed in democracy, not theocracy.

The Wall Street crash, 24 October 1929

IN FOREIGN affairs, during the period when he was building his political party, his principal concern was inevitably Anglo-Irish relations, and the righting of what he regarded as the wrongs of the 1922 Treaty. However he also hoped to re-establish his country's, his party's and indeed his own political base of support in the United States. But with the stock market crash of 1929, and the resultant depression, Americans, even Irish Americans, had little time or money for the affairs of their ever more remote cousins across the ocean. Sympathy, often of a sentimental sort only, remained. Henceforth American political support for the Irish cause was to be minimal and at times, particularly during and immediately after the Second World War, non-existent and was even to be replaced on occasion by hostility. With the assimilation of the Irish into the American way of life, and into American patriotism, the loyalty to the old country dwindled into the singing of songs and an occasional holiday in Ireland. And of course to the great St Patrick's Day parades in New York and elsewhere.

*De Valera reviewing the Irish Army,
Phoenix Park, Dublin, 1936*

*De Valera at the taking over of Spike
Island in Cork Harbour, one of the
'Treaty Ports', in 1938*

THE so-called Tariff War, which began in 1933, did not end with a 'Tariff Peace' in 1938: however, agreements more or less satisfactory both to London and to Dublin were reached, tariffs on both sides were substantially reduced, and a greater degree of amity prevailed between the two governments than at any time since the signing of the Treaty. For Ireland this had been an expensive operation, both in the obvious financial sense, but more important in the high incidence of emigration that the resultant poverty had brought about. Yet there were two very positive politico-economic gains. The first was that this form of economic nationalism had severed some of the dominant links that Britain had hitherto preserved in Ireland. The second was that this brief period of semi-autarchy had necessitated a far wider diversification of Irish agriculture and had also served as a spur to Irish industrialisation. Without the Tariff War and the concomitant need for much greater economic self-reliance, for which Eamon de Valera and his government were directly responsible, Ireland would have remained in pawn to Britain and would scarcely have been in a position to pursue its own policy of neutrality during the Second World War.

The Tariff War was but one aspect of Eamon de Valera's determination to reinforce and extend Irish sovereignty, which meant in effect maximum independence of Britain in economic, military, constitutional and even linguistic matters. The Tariff War was closely connected with the issue of the so-called Treaty Ports, British naval bases in the Free State, and indeed the return of the Treaty Ports really brought an end to the Tariff War. As the storm clouds gathered over Europe, the issue of Irish neutrality in a future war became one of prime importance both to the Free State and to the United Kingdom. One of the reasons de Valera advanced to the British for ending the Tariff War was the need for Ireland to be in a position to buy armaments for the defence of Irish territory. This argument appealed both to the British government and to the British Chiefs of Staff who had no wish to find themselves responsible for the defence of Ireland.

De Valera on the occasion of the enactment of the new constitution, 1937

AFTER the general election of 1934 which Fianna Fáil won with a greatly increased majority, de Valera had far more freedom of action. Almost immediately he set about re-drafting the Irish Constitution. The principal amendments were, perhaps characteristically, symbolic. In the new Constitution there was no mention of the Crown, the Governor-General or the British Commonwealth. Thus the new Constitution made Ireland more or less a Republic *de facto*. *De jure* this was not to be achieved until 1949, ironically enough during one of the brief periods when Ireland had a coalition government in which de Valera played no part. The 1937 Constitution also clipped ruthlessly the already limited powers of the Upper House, the *Seanad* or Senate. The Irish legislature became in effect a one chamber parliament.

De Valera addressing the League of Nations, in the 1930s

Anthony Eden, M.P., at Government Buildings, 6 September 1938

AS PRIME Minister of the Irish Free State, de Valera also kept in his own hands the portfolio of External Affairs. In the 1930s, as before the Civil War, he believed that he and he alone had the stature to speak for Ireland in the concert of the nations. And he availed himself to the full of the most prominent platform then available to the representative of a small country, namely the League of Nations. He went to Geneva every year, from 1932 until the war killed the League. On his first visit he found himself, fortuitously, President of the Assembly. On the first occasion he delivered an oration warning the League of the dangers to its very existence posed by the recent Japanese aggression in China. Like all Cassandras, this warning did not make him popular with his fellow delegates, but it drew a great deal of attention in parts of the world where Ireland was unknown or forgotten. He spoke each year, while the League became increasingly moribund politically. In 1938 he urged a Peace Conference *before,* instead of after, the holocaust that all saw coming.

Undoubtedly these international speeches did much to enhance his reputation in his own country, for the Irish were gratified to see their leader assume the role, and be accepted, as a global statesman. Undoubtedly too they did much for Ireland's status in the world, in that they made it plain for all to see that Ireland was now an independent power, in its own right, with its own voice and its own policies. It was precisely this that he wished to achieve.

I.R.A. bomb outrages in the London tube, 3 February 1939

CO-INCIDENTAL to, and in part resulting from, the Tariff War, anti-Catholic riots broke out again in Northern Ireland in 1933, reaching a climax in 1935 when about a dozen people were killed in three weeks. De Valera was, as he had always been, committed to a peaceful solution to the Northern Irish and Partition issue, a commitment which could only be reinforced by his League of Nations activities. He limited himself to verbal protests.

Thus the more extreme nationalists in Ireland, on both sides of the Border, veered towards the illegal I.R.A. which for the first time since the Civil War enjoyed a considerable accretion both of strength and of morale. In 1936 the I.R.A. decided on an active campaign of physical force, principally bombing, to be directed both against the British in their own country and against the authorities, particularly the Royal Ulster Constabulary, in Northern Ireland. Between then and the outbreak of war the I.R.A. did considerable damage, physically to the British and, morally, to the Irish themselves. Lives were lost. Although I.R.A. leaders were arrested in the Free State, the de Valera government did not believe that it had sufficient powers, as the I.R.A. grew both more efficient and more ruthless. In June 1939 the 'Offences against the State Act' was passed, the I.R.A. was declared an illegal organisation, and trial by military court replaced trial by jury. In September with the outbreak of the Second World War, the 'Emergency Powers Bill' gave the government yet greater strength to deal with illegal organisations, and as amended, in January 1940, it gave the government the right to intern suspected persons without trial. Shortly after this the Curragh Camp became a sort of concentration camp, in which were interned not only Allied and German military persons but also proven or even suspected activists of the I.R.A.

De Valera was too shrewd and experienced a politician to permit the existence, on Irish soil, of an armed force, alternative and probably hostile to the armed forces of the State, particularly during a long period of major international crisis.

De Valera, c. 1943 (above)

'Unity' Meeting, 1940 (right)

Mr de Valera receiving the Seal of Office as Taoiseach from Dr Douglas
Hyde, President of Ireland, 1944 (below)

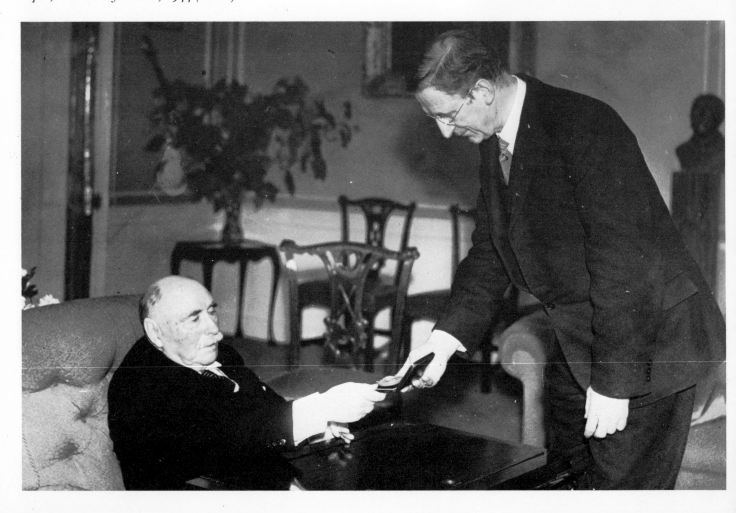

IT WOULD seem probable that no independent Irish government could have chosen any other policy save neutrality in 1939 and survived. It was a benevolent form of neutrality, benevolent that is to the Western Allies. But beyond benevolence (a blind eye to the 'escape' of interned R.A.F. or U.S.A.A.F. pilots; no hindrance to Irishmen volunteering for the British forces; thorough and highly efficient neutralisation of German espionage and sabotage endeavours; continued imprisonment of I.R.A. men), beyond all this de Valera would not go, neither when subjected to a measure of economic blackmail by the British for the return of the Treaty Ports, nor when bullied politically by the British and the Americans at a later stage of the war. Even at the very end, dignity forbad entry on the Allied side, as was done by Turkey and others in search of post-war benefits. At a cost which can be roughly assessed in financial, but not in moral or social, terms, Ireland remained neutral throughout. This long, extremely complicated, and at times dangerous manoeuvre was undoubtedly one for which de Valera was superbly equipped, for he was never the man to seize the opportune at the cost of the absolute. His acute and abstract brain, combined with his steely patriotic and moral fibre, enabled him to steer the Irish ship of state safely through those long and turbulent years, and to take his people with him.

Mr de Valera replies on 16 May 1945 to Prime Minister Winston Churchill's criticisms of Irish policy

IN THE euphoria of victory, on 13 May 1945, Winston Churchill broadcast a speech in which he took a sideswipe at Irish neutrality, mentioning de Valera by name. He said:

'With a restraint and poise to which, I venture to say, history will find few parallels, His Majesty's Government never laid a violent hand upon them [the Irish], though at times it would have been quite easy and quite natural, and we left the de Valera government to frolic with the German and later with the Japanese representatives to their hearts' content.' Three days later the Irishman replied, also over the radio. It was a long speech. Among many other highly pertinent remarks, he said:

'It is indeed hard for the strong to be just to the weak. But acting justly always has its rewards. By resisting his temptation in this instance, Mr Churchill, instead of adding another horrid chapter to the already bloodstained record of the relations between Ireland and his country, has advanced the cause of international morality an important step . . . Could he not find in his heart the generosity to acknowledge that there is a small nation which stood alone not for one year or two, but for several hundred years against aggression; that endured spoliations, was clubbed many times into insensibility, but that each time on returning to consciousness took up the fight anew; a small nation that could never be got to accept defeat and has never surrendered her soul?'

The only family group of Eamon and Sinéad de Valera and all their children. Standing (left to right): Ruarí, Vivion, Eamon, Brian; sitting (left to right): Máirín, Sinéad and Eamon de Valera, Emer; and kneeling in front: Terry. Brian died shortly after this picture was taken in 1936

MR AND MRS de Valera had seven children, born between 1910 and 1922. Of these, six survived, one son, Brian, dying in 1936 at the age of twenty as the result of a riding accident. Brian, and the eldest son, Vivion, inherited a measure of their father's mathematical brilliance. All the surviving children did well in life, three of them becoming professors and one marrying a professor, one a well-known doctor, another a leading solicitor. Their modesty and intellectual distinction have been passed on to his grandchildren and, no doubt, to his great-grandchildren as well. A 'dynasty' would be the wrong word. But Eamon de Valera played a very major part in the creation of modern Ireland: for many years he guided and guarded his country: and he and his wife, Sinéad, gave it one of its most distinguished families.

In the 1930s he had moved to Blackrock, to a modest but comfortable home in which to bring up his younger children, with a pleasant garden, cats and usually a dog. There he lived until his election to the Presidency in 1959 entailed a move to Arus an Uachtaráin, the handsome Presidential, formerly Vice-Regal, Lodge in Phoenix Park. This did not altogether please Mrs de Valera to whose modest and indeed retiring nature the Blackrock house was a more congenial home.

Although during the hectic years, 1916–24, she had, during her husband's long absences, to act both as mother and father to their children, she never attempted to usurp his position as head of the household. It was a happy home and, by all accounts, a gay one too. With his family, according to their memories of childhood, de Valera entirely shed the armour of austerity which he donned in public. There was much laughter, music and the reading or recital of poems.

In London with Ernest Bevin, John Strachey and the Prime Minister, Mr Clement Attlee

Speaking at Ennis, 21 May 1944

UNTIL the general election of 1948, Eamon de Valera remained Taoiseach, though Fianna Fáil lacked an absolute majority in the Dáil. In international affairs, once the immediate aftermath of the war was over, political currents in the Western world were very favourable to the course that he wished his country to pursue. The revulsion against totalitarianism, whether of the Nazi, Fascist and soon enough of the Communist variety, brought the Christian Democrats to power in Italy and a little later in Germany too. A Christian Democrat is precisely what de Valera had always been. The Communist party in Ireland was negligible, the government, clergy and people profoundly hostile to that ideology; therefore when the United States and the United Kingdom quite quickly recognised their new enemy, Ireland, which had never had any diplomatic and only very slight commercial relationships either with the Soviet Union or now with its newly won satellite Communist states in Eastern Europe, found that its wartime neutrality was quickly forgiven by the great powers. While preserving military neutrality, in that Ireland adhered neither to the Brussels Treaty of 1948, nor to the North Atlantic Treaty Organization of the following year, in economic and quasi-political fields Ireland was entirely acceptable to such bodies as the Organization for European Economic Co-operation and the Council of Europe. Later Ireland was to play a prominent part in the affairs of the United Nations. In fact, Ireland's enhanced international status was firmly based on the foundations that de Valera had laid before and during the war, and it was on these that he and his successors proceeded to build.

Relations with Britain were eased by the electorate's dismissal of Winston Churchill and the formation of a Labour Government in the summer of 1945. Superficially at least, British Socialists being successors to the almost vanished Liberals have usually been better disposed to Irish aspiration than have Conservative-Unionists. Here much was done to smooth Anglo-Irish relations, though despite Britain's rapid withdrawal from Empire nothing was achieved to alleviate the Partition issue in Ireland.

John A. Costello, 1891–

Seán MacBride, 1904–

IN DOMESTIC affairs the first post-war de Valera administration was happily situated, both for economic and for political reasons.

To ensure maximum economic stability, wages and prices had been pegged throughout the war, on the whole successfully. The crisis passed and the people would no longer accept such controls, a point of view with which Fianna Fáil could only agree. Their removal, however, led inevitably to a measure of inflation. Strikes ensued, in particular among those employed by the State such as the schoolteachers. The government, itself short of money, tried to curb inflation by restrictions within the public sector, but with little success. As always, and often correctly, the nation's economic ills were blamed on the government in office. The farmers, too, formed their own political party, hostile to the government, and won a few bye-elections.

Secondly, the release of the I.R.A. men from the Curragh launched into political life a fairly large number of embittered men, often with considerable political acumen. To them were added many nationalists who disapproved of de Valera's friendly attitude towards Britain, his failure to deal with the Partition issue, and his apparent acceptance of the Free State's status, even with his 1937 Constitution, and its indeterminate British links; they wanted a Republic, and at once. They united, temporarily, behind Seán MacBride an intense patriot and former I.R.A. leader, with a great Irish name, for the British had shot his father in 1916 and his mother was Maud Gonne. Finally, Labour and its principal support, the trade unions, were gaining in strength. All these forces were eroding both the Republican and the left-wing elements within Fianna Fáil. Though these new parties and groupings had little in common with the main opposition party, Fine Gael, they were prepared to make any sort of an alliance in order to topple Fianna Fáil.

In the 1948 election Fianna Fáil failed to win a majority, and the opposition formed the first Coalition Government, headed by John A. Costello with Seán MacBride at the Ministry for External Affairs. This took de Valera by surprise for until the very last minute he had assumed that Labour would prefer a Coalition with his own party. The Coalition that came about was in essence a negation, a politically grotesque compromise of incompatible views. However, as a good democrat, de Valera went quietly into opposition.

Celebrations during Easter Week, 1949, to mark the coming into operation of the Republic of Ireland Act. Mr de Valera and his colleagues did not participate

Mr de Valera with Pandit Nehru in India, 1948

LEADERSHIP of an Opposition implies, among much else, an intensive playing of party politics. This was not a role for which so olympian a figure as de Valera was well cast. However the Coalition Government was such a ramshackle, such a ragbag of conflicting policies, that his task was a comparatively easy one and Fianna Fáil returned to office after the general election of 1951.

The declaration of the Republic in 1949 was really the only major act by the Costello government. Though as always a staunch republican, de Valera opposed this constitutional change, principally on the grounds that it would make the re-unification of all Ireland more difficult. Indeed the reaction of the British Labour Party's government bore him out: the Ireland Act, which passed through the United Kingdom parliament immediately after the declaration of the Republic, stated categorically that there could be no change, ever, to the status of the Six Counties without the approval of the Northern Irish parliament. Since Stormont was the mouthpiece of the Unionist Party, itself dominated and manipulated by the Orange Order, this meant in effect—never.

For reasons both of taste and of policy de Valera objected strongly to the somewhat ostentatious celebrations that marked the inauguration of the Republic. Ostentation was never his style and he believed and said that such celebrations and parades should be reserved against the day of re-unification and the declaration of a thirty-two-county Republic.

Meanwhile, out of office, he had more time for travel. He visited India in 1949. He campaigned vigorously in the 1951 election. Fianna Fáil was victorious, while Seán MacBride's party was decimated, in part owing to the hostility of the Church which disapproved of the Coalition's social policies, principally those concerning medical matters. De Valera was Taoiseach once again. Yet this was an unsatisfactory government since he had to rely on the support of independent members of the Dáil. Fianna Fáil, though much the largest party, had no absolute majority.

Dr McQuaid, for many years Archbishop of Dublin. He is said to have advised Mr de Valera on certain religious aspects of the 1937 Constitution

THE FIRST task of the new government, which held office from 1951 to 1954 was, in his view, to halt the inflation that had gathered momentum under the Coalition by a return to more traditional economic policies. Conservative economics and balanced budgets do not win popularity in modern times. Only when inflation is getting completely and obviously out of hand will the people accept tough anti-inflationary measures, and this was not the case in Ireland at that time.

Secondly 'welfare' benefits in the new Republic were lagging well behind those prevailing in the United Kingdom, including of course Northern Ireland. Not only was this unfair to the citizens of the Republic but was also a further divisive element between North and South. Health was a particularly neglected field, the cost of medicine and medical attention a real hardship among the poor in the Republic, while in the Six Counties these were free. The hierarchy (for whom Archbishop McQuaid was a spokesman and who had long been close to de Valera) disapproved of the Coalition's Health Bill, which the Minister for Health Dr Noel Browne proposed and argued forcefully; yet the Fianna Fáil government introduced a basically similar bill in 1953, to be greeted with almost exactly the same reaction from the same source. However, de Valera was in a far stronger position to deal with the bishops than his predecessors had been, and smoothed their ruffled feathers while refusing to let them veto his policies. The bill became law, and something was done to ameliorate the plight of the impoverished sick in Ireland. The electoral system—a very complicated form of proportional representation—was in de Valera's view becoming increasingly unsatisfactory. Though it ensured the representation of minority groups and interests inside the Dáil, this in turn had led, particularly since 1943, to a proliferation of ephemeral, unstable political parties and weak government. De Valera was well aware of what a menace such an electoral system had been to the French Third Republic and was now to the Fourth. However, his government was not strong enough for basic constitutional reform. He went to the country in 1954, his party was defeated, and until 1957 he was once again the leader of the Opposition to a Coalition Government which proved no more homogeneous nor effective than the last one.

Mr de Valera in Zürich, 1936, where he went to consult an eye specialist

BY NOW Eamon de Valera was almost completely blind. His eyesight had begun to fail badly, double vision being the first most notable symptom, in the late 1920s and early 1930s. By 1936 this had reached a point where he had to have a major operation in Zürich. A few years later he was operated on for cataracts, and his sight was again temporarily restored. When his government fell in 1948 he was sorting papers on the floor, stooping of course, and his retinas became detached. Six operations in Utrecht gave him a measure of peripheral vision and the ability to distinguish large objects, but henceforth he could not read. However with his extreme determination, aided by a prodigious capacity for memorisation, he found that he could still lead his Party both in and out of office. In Dáil debates he was able to quote from memory complex facts and figures. And in 1957, for the first time since the war, Fianna Fáil won a general election that gave his party an overall majority in the Dáil. For the last time, de Valera was Taoiseach once again.

Dr T. K. Whitaker, among Ireland's foremost official economic experts

The Treaty Ports

HE WAS now in a sufficiently strong position to set in motion those electoral reforms that he regarded as essential to the security of parliamentary democracy in the Republic of Ireland. Briefly, these would have brought about a one member constituency system similar to that prevailing in the United Kingdom and, of course, in Ireland before 1922. The bill was bitterly fought, and once defeated by a single vote, in the Dáil, for the opposition parties saw it not only as their death warrant, if they were small, but also as a device to ensure a permanent Fianna Fáil government for all the foreseeable future. Furthermore the Irish constitution required that such a change be approved by the people voting in a national plebiscite or referendum. Another bitter campaign was fought and in due course the people voted against the proposed changes (as was to happen to another Fianna Fáil government when it appealed to the people on the same issue in 1970). But by the time the referendum was held, in June of 1959, Eamon de Valera was no longer Taoiseach.

The other, and ultimately far more successful initiative by his government during his brief, last premiership was a basic reappraisal of the whole Irish economy by Dr T. K. Whitaker then Secretary to the Department of Finance. With de Valera's agreement the anonymity of the report, and the resultant 'five years' plan' was waived in regard to this distinguished civil servant. The Irish economy, by a judicious combination of protection, subsidy and the encouragement of foreign capital investment, prospered greatly, much poverty was eliminated, and the emigration rate fell.

Finally, the I.R.A. launched a cross-border campaign, directed principally against the Royal Ulster Constabulary and customs' posts north of the Border, such as Killeen, which lasted from 1956 to 1962. The I.R.A. leaders attempted to win Mr de Valera's approval of this campaign while he was in opposition. This he categorically refused to give, repeating yet again that physical force would never provide a solution to the problem of the Border.

De Valera becomes President of the Republic of Ireland, 1959

IN 1959 President Seán T. O'Kelly's second term of office as President of Ireland was due to end. According to the Constitution he could not be elected to a third. Various persons in the inner councils of Fianna Fáil had approached the Taoiseach, in late 1958, that he might care to put his name forward as contester for the Presidency in the election for that office which was to fall due in the summer of 1959.

He held his counsel, but at a meeting of the Fianna Fáil Parliamentary Party, early in 1959, he announced his intention to resign both from office and from leadership of that Party. As for the matter of the Presidency he was, he said, 'completely in the hands of the Party'. His decision caused consternation, grief, even tears among many of his followers. 'The Chief', as they called him, had led the Party since he first created it, over a third of a century ago, in opposition for some twelve years, in office for twenty-one of the last twenty-seven. From a band of rebels, most of whom in 1926 had only recently been released from prison, he had created the most stream-lined and efficient political machine that had existed on Irish soil at least since Parnell's time. (The Sinn Féin that Arthur Griffith had created and that he had led during 'the Troubles' was a national movement rather than a political party.) Nor was there any obvious heir of his stature in sight though Seán Lemass was obviously the principal claimant to leadership of the Party. It would be no exaggeration to say that the imminent departure of 'The Chief' frightened, if only temporarily, some of his followers. For even if he were elected Head of State, as President he must be above party politics.

He was in fact elected President on the same day that the people of Ireland rejected his electoral reforms. As with so much of his political career, this was another bitter-sweet verdict by his compatriots. On 25 June 1959, he became President of Ireland in a ceremony held in St Patrick's Hall, Dublin Castle.

De Valera hands over the Seal of Office as Taoiseach to Seán Lemass. Centre, Seán T. O'Kelly, the retiring President

HE WAS seventy-six years of age when he moved into the beautiful presidential residence, Arus an Uachtaráin, in the Phoenix Park. Seán Lemass succeeded him as Taoiseach and as the leader of Fianna Fáil. With his usual tact and charm President de Valera had already made the transfer of power to his successor as easy as possible. No fissures appeared within Fianna Fáil as was to happen when, in his turn, Seán Lemass handed over the leadership to Mr Jack Lynch in 1967.

President de Valera was intensely conscious of the dignity of his high office, of his responsibility to all the Irish people including those living north of the Border, and of his constitutional position above party politics. This last consideration was in some ways made easier for him during both his Presidencies (for he was re-elected, though with a much smaller majority, in 1966 to serve a further seven-year term) by the fact that Fianna Fáil was in office throughout, that the members of the government had almost invariably served under him in past cabinets, and that he was thus available for discussion of proposed legislation with old colleagues. There was a minimum of friction between the President and the Government.

However, should he regard a bill as passed by the Dáil and sent to him for signature as being perhaps unconstitutional he was quite capable of calling a Council of State and, if need be, of referring it to the Supreme Court. But so close was his relationship with Seán Lemass and later with Mr Lynch, so well-oiled the Fianna Fáil machine, that such presidential intervention was very rare indeed. Differences of opinion were usually, indeed almost invariably, resolved before a bill was submitted to the Dáil, not after it had been passed for his signature. So far as is known, he did not initiate policy, but even in extreme old age he remained 'The Chief'.

President de Valera with President Kennedy at Arus an Uachtaráin

With ex-President de Gaulle at Arus an Uachtaráin, 1967

ONE OF his duties as Head of State was to act as host to Ireland's most distinguished visitors. He is seen on the opposite page with the late President John F. Kennedy of the United States. In 1951 Ireland's application for membership of the U.N. (not automatic in 1945, because of Ireland's wartime neutrality) had been vetoed by the Soviet Union. But almost as soon as Ireland was at last admitted, in 1955, and particularly during and after de Valera's last premiership, his country played a role quite disproportionate to its population in United Nations affairs. Because of his successful neutrality policies in the past and present, Irish troops were much in demand for peace-keeping activities in the Congo and Cyprus, for example. This in turn was a logical extrapolation of de Valera's League of Nations activities before the war, and a source of pride to his fellow-countrymen. The visit of John F. Kennedy to Ireland in 1963 gave the Irish the very greatest popular satisfaction. They did not regard the first Irish-American Roman Catholic President as a foreigner, but as one of themselves coming home triumphant. Though aged eighty-one and blind, President de Valera travelled to Washington for President Kennedy's funeral a few months after this photograph was taken. Indeed his travels as President were considerable. He visited both Pope John in Rome, in 1962, and attended the coronation of Pope Paul in that city a few years later. The list of his distinguished guests in Ireland is endless. General de Gaulle sought a rest in Ireland when he resigned the Presidency of France in 1967. For once de Valera found himself, physically at least, overtopped by a statesman of his own generation whose career and whose patriotic vision had in many ways run parallel to his own.

In 1966 Mr Jack Lynch, here seen on the Preside... right, succeeded Seán Lemass as Taoiseach (above...

Trouble begins again in Northern Ireland in 196... Members of the Royal Ulster Constabulary in ac... (left)

Trouble brewing. A member of the Orange Order... passing a military post in Derry (below)

IN 1966, with the retirement of Seán Lemass from active politics, he swore in Mr Jack Lynch's first cabinet.

Two years later the troubles in the North broke out yet again. Riots in Derry were soon to spread, with mounting violence, to Belfast and other urban centres in the Six Counties, with unpleasant repercussions south of the Border as well.

With impeccable correctitude, the President of the Republic made no public comment on the miseries unfolding in what he had always regarded as an integral part of Ireland. It is not hard to guess, however, how saddened and perhaps angered he must have been to hear of such renewed sectarian violence in his own country: for his inability to re-unite Ireland has been undoubtedly the greatest personal failure, as it has perhaps been the supreme ambition, of his whole, full, long political life. Yet perhaps this is outweighed by his many real and tangible successes. The Ireland that he leaves behind him is utterly different from the Ireland that he had first served as a volunteer soldier in 1913. The changes are in great measure stamped with his idealism, his integrity, and indeed his personality. That other influences, some considerably less attractive, contributed to the creation of modern Ireland is beyond dispute. But without Eamon de Valera's long service Ireland would not be the country that Ireland now is.

President de Valera on his ninetieth birthday,
14 October 1972

Signing the Instrument of Ratification of the Treaty of
Accession to the E.E.C. with the Taoiseach, Jack Lynch,
on 13 December 1972.

1972 was the year in which President de Valera celebrated his ninetieth birthday and was also his last full year in office. It was also and without doubt the most tragic year in Irish history for half a century, but upon the events and decisions of that year he refrained, as he had before, from comment. Yet in several ways it saw the ideals that had inspired him for so long vanish one by one.

As we have noted, his greatest ambition, since that long-distant day when he swore an oath at the Rotunda Rink, had been to see a free, united, thirty-two county Irish Christian democratic republic. It was for this ideal that he had refused the Treaty of 1922. Yet back in office, external events in 1939 had compelled him to enforce against his own old comrades undemocratic methods of internment for the extreme republicans. The great increase in violence in the North that had begun in 1969 and that mounted *crescendo* throughout the following years, at last compelled the British in 1972 however reluctantly, to disband the democratically elected government at Stormont and to impose direct British rule in the six counties of Ulster, backed by ever more massive military force.

Murder and bombings on an increasing scale produced in the North a bitterness far exceeding that of 1914 and perhaps without equal force since the seventeenth century. In the Republic a measure of initial, traditional sympathy for the gunmen of the I.R.A. almost entirely evaporated when that organization set about the terror-bombing of civilian centres. It became apparent to all that a united Ireland could only come about as a gift from the British. It became equally apparent that this gift, when it is made, will be received with great reluctance by almost all Irishmen everywhere, and will bring with it appalling problems of the utmost complexity. Re-unification is unlikely to take place in President de Valera's lifetime. One of his major ambitions has pre-deceased him.

Another ambition was to see the sort of Ireland of which he dreamed: an essentially rural but balanced economy, not perhaps the mythical island of 'saints and scholars', but nevertheless a firmly Christian and very individualistic society, its individualism to find its most obvious expression in the re-creation of the Irish tongue which remains, officially, the country's first language. However, as a vernacular, Irish is spoken naturally in those parts of the West which are becoming increasingly depopulated while the English-speaking east coast, particularly the Dublin area, is not only being physically rebuilt on the English model —often by British capital—but is becoming socially and morally less and less distinguishable from Britain.

The social force of religion is also on the decline and in a referendum held in December 1972 the people voted away the 'special position' assigned by de Valera in his 1937 Constitution to the Roman Catholic Church.

Earlier in the same year in another referendum, the Irish people had voted for membership of the European Economic Community. Though theoretically a sovereign state, who can doubt that within the Community Irish interests must be subservient to British ones where the two collide, economically in the first place but ultimately politically as well? Was this vote not the popular negation of 'Sinn Féin' for which de Valera struggled so long? And what of the neutrality for which he sacrificed so much?

Finally, late in 1972, the Fianna Fáil government rushed through legislation which gives the police powers of detention and evidence against any person whom they believe might be a danger to the State. These powers, directed primarily against the I.R.A., have, at the time of writing, not been abused. There is, however, no temporal limit attached to them, and thus no telling how some future government might not use them.

Old men shall dream dreams . . . If the Ireland of today is indelibly stamped with de Valera's personality, it is most certainly not the country of which the young man dreamed, and for which the middle-aged man fought, worked and sacrificed so much morally as well as in material terms. If there is glory, and there *is* glory, there is also here much tragedy and, above all, an irony that seems to many Irishmen almost intolerably painful.

He dreams of the past, no doubt, more than of the future, but for the present perhaps the best epitaph would be the closing line of Alfred de Vigny's *La Mort du Loup*. That it is in French may be relevant and perhaps, but improbably, hopeful for the new Union.

Puis, après, comme moi, souffre et meurs sans parler.

INDEX